The Elective Carnegie Community Engagement Classification

Campus Compact is a national coalition of colleges and universities committed to the public purposes of higher education. Campus Compact publications focus on practical strategies for campuses to put civic education and community engagement into action. Please visit http://compact.org for more information.

Campus Compact

The Elective Carnegie Community Engagement Classification

Constructing a Successful Application for First-Time and Re-Classification Applicants

Edited by

JOHN SALTMARSH AND
MATHEW B. JOHNSON

Foreword by
ANDREW J. SELIGSOHN

Campus Compact

BOSTON, MASSACHUSETTS
Distributed by Stylus Publishing, LLC.

COPYRIGHT © 2018 BY CAMPUS COMPACT

Published by Campus Compact
45 Temple Place
Boston, MA 02111

Library of Congress Cataloging-in-Publication Data
The CIP data for this text has been applied for.

13-digit ISBN: 978-1-945459-13-9 (cloth)
13-digit ISBN: 978-1-945459-14-6 (paperback)
13-digit ISBN: 978-1-945459-15-3 (library networkable e-edition)
13-digit ISBN: 978-1-945459-16-0 (consumer e-edition)

Printed in the United States of America

All first editions printed on acid-free paper
that meets the American National Standards Institute

Z39-48 Standard.

Bulk Purchases

Quantity discounts are available for use in workshops and for staff development.

Call 1-800-232-0223

First Edition, 2018

To Amy Driscoll, for her vision and leadership in bringing together an often unruly group of scholars and practitioners to create a framework that has set common standards for institutionalizing quality community engagement in American higher education.

To Howard R. Swearer (1932–1991), the 15th president of Brown University, serving from 1977 to 1988. In 1985, Swearer was one of the founding presidents of Campus Compact. Under his leadership, in 1987, Brown became one of the first campuses in the nation to establish a formal center for public service. In 1992, the Center for Public Service was named the Howard R. Swearer Center for Public Service.

CONTENTS

Early in 2010, I found myself sitting in the office of Chancellor Wendell Pritchett of Rutgers University–Camden (Rutgers–Camden). Wendell had recently hired me to lead the university's civic engagement efforts, and we were meeting to decide whether to seek the Carnegie Classification for Community Engagement in the 2010 cycle.

Both of us were quite new to the university, as Wendell had begun as chancellor only a few months earlier. Neither of us had engaged directly with the Carnegie process before. We knew neither what the process would entail nor whether our university was going to be in a position to earn the classification. We concluded in our brief discussion that the very worst that could happen is that we would learn a lot about where Rutgers–Camden was and where we needed to go. Wendell had identified fulfilling the university's public role in the city of Camden as a major priority of his administration, so that worst-case scenario looked pretty good. We decided to go for it.

Over the following months, I brought together a group of staff and faculty engaged in teaching, research, and partnerships that connected Rutgers–Camden with communities beyond the campus. Because the Office of Civic Engagement was a new entity on campus, these engaged scholars and practitioners were not linked to each other, and most had little familiarity with the work of the others. Together we began to fill out a picture of the community engagement landscape at Rutgers–Camden. As we did, we made several discoveries.

First, we discovered that Rutgers–Camden supported an extraordinarily rich landscape of partnerships. In all of the university's colleges and in a wide variety of centers and institutes, Rutgers–Camden people were working alongside community partners to advance public goods. These partnerships were achieving impact for community residents in areas that mattered to them.

Second, we learned that relatively few students—and notably few undergraduates—were strongly connected to these partnerships. Much of Rutgers–Camden's partnership work was based in centers and institutes that were distant from the experience of most students. Many of the people leading the work did not have faculty appointments. Community engagement was happening *at* the university but it was not fully *of* the university in the sense of being embedded in the core teaching and research components of the institution. An extraordinary learning opportunity was being missed.

Third, we found that there was no ongoing infrastructure to examine how well we were doing the work and how we could do it better. We had few structures to bring the voices of community residents and partners into our decision-making. We had no ongoing assessment that would help us make sense of the variety of programs and projects and how they did or did not fit together to build a better Camden.

When we submitted our documentation framework for the Carnegie Classification for Community Engagement in 2010, our team was not especially optimistic about the formal response. But we were optimistic about the outcomes of the process. We felt we had emerged from our shared work with a clear sense of what we needed to do to deepen our impact for students and for communities and to make the university's public mission an integral part of its practice. In that cycle, we did not earn the classification, and the reviewers' rationale aligned with our own sense of where we needed to go.

Even before we were notified that we had not received the classification, we were hard at work in pursuit of a change agenda. We built a Faculty Fellows program to increase capacity to integrate community engagement into the curriculum. We created an Engaged Civic Learning course designation that became integrated into the general education requirements. We launched a Bonner Leader program to cultivate a core group of highly engaged students to serve as organizers and exemplars for their peers. We built a working group of faculty researchers to advise the Office of Civic Engagement on approaches to assessment, out of which came a comprehensive assessment strategy. We developed consistent venues for community voice and participation. We designed and redesigned partnerships to facilitate the integration of teaching, research, and action in pursuit of stronger and healthier communities.

By the time the 2015 cycle rolled around, we knew we were ready, and Rutgers–Camden earned the Carnegie Classification for Community Engagement. Far more importantly, Rutgers–Camden is now an exemplary engaged university—in part because my colleagues and I took advantage of the opportunity presented by the Carnegie Classification to take a serious look at our work and challenge ourselves to do better and achieve more.

I hope this volume helps colleges and universities maximize the learning and development accomplished through the Carnegie Classification process. Its chapters, and the lessons contained therein, apply to every type of institution—two year, four year, public, private, faith based, rural, urban, large, small. Like the Carnegie Classification process itself, these chapters are an invitation to begin an ongoing conversation on your campus and with your community about your institution's mission to serve the public, how well you are achieving it, and your opportunities for doing better. The Carnegie Classification process asks you to take a look back—to see what you have created and how it has worked. In the best case, institutions will connect this retrospective work with forward-looking efforts such as Campus Compact's Civic Action Plan initiative, linking an informed understanding of how far you have come with an affirmative vision of where you hope to go.

The Carnegie Classification for Community Engagement is not an end in itself. No one's life is automatically improved by the achievement of the classification by any institution. But if the people pursuing the classification are motivated by a desire to achieve ever-greater impact and are willing to be honest with themselves and each other about how they are doing, the process can provide institutions with a powerful opportunity to understand where they stand and to identify a path forward. This volume can help get that process started.

Andrew J. Seligsohn
President, Campus Compact

Chapter One

AN INTRODUCTION TO THE ELECTIVE CARNEGIE COMMUNITY ENGAGEMENT CLASSIFICATION

John Saltmarsh and Mathew B. Johnson

Background and Purpose

By the late 1990s, community engagement in American higher education, by its many names,[1] had developed to the point where colleges and universities were attempting to more deeply embed it in practices across the campus. They pursued a process of institutionalization that meant attending to and aligning practices, structures, and policies across the campus. Institutions founded on the purpose of generating and disseminating knowledge in the context of education's relationship to democracy thus enhanced the pursuit of their mission through engagement. Institutionalizing community engagement meant focusing on the ways in which (a) engagement impacted the educational experience of students; (b) engagement needed to be integrated into faculty scholarly experience—teaching, research and creative activity, and service; and (c) engagement required budgets, professional staffing, and other infrastructure to be successful.

The *Presidents' Declaration on the Civic Responsibility of Higher Education* (Campus Compact, 1999) called for campuses to promote "recognition of civic responsibility in accreditation procedures, Carnegie classifications, and national rankings, and to work with governors, state legislators, and state higher education offices on expectations for civic engagement in public systems" (p. 2). One of the coauthors of the declaration was Thomas Ehrlich, a senior scholar at the Carnegie Foundation for the Advancement of Teaching.

The Carnegie Foundation has been classifying institutions of higher education since the early 1970s. The foundation has historically been committed to the improvement of undergraduate education in the United States, and the Carnegie Classification (Basic Classification) was created to organize institutions by mission differentiation, degree level, and specialization. All accredited two- and four-year colleges and universities have a Carnegie Classification. The rich heterogeneity of higher education in the United States has been a hallmark of its innovation and excellence. In the early 2000s, the foundation sought to design a new "Elective" Classification for Community Engagement. The Elective Classification differs from the Basic Classification, which reports descriptive characteristics of the institution gathered through publicly available data sets without any assessment of those characteristics. The Elective Classification gathers data specifically provided by the campus and unavailable through other means and is intended to assist in a process of institutional change through self-assessment and national review to improve the educational effectiveness of the campus. With this Elective Classification depending on voluntary participation by institutions, the foundation created a "special-purpose classification" that would "open the possibility for involving only those institutions with special commitments in the area of community engagement" (McCormick & Zhao, 2005, p. 56).

Amy Driscoll, a scholar with deep experience in community engagement and assessment at both Portland State University and California State University, Monterey Bay, joined the foundation to guide the development of the framework and drew from earlier institutionalization rubrics for service-learning and community engagement (Furco, 1999; Holland, 2000; Hollander, Saltmarsh, & Zlotkowski, 2001; Kecskes & Muyllaert, 1997), as well as the input of leading scholars. She worked with representatives from 13 campuses to pilot the framework in 2005. The creation of the Community Engagement Classification was seen by some as emblematic of a much broader "counterbalancing" shift in higher education. Gary Rhoades (2009), general secretary of the American Association of University Professors (AAUP), wrote that "if the effect of Carnegie's efforts (and those of Dupont Circle and AAUP) in the first three quarters of the 20th century was to inscribe in academic structures and in the consciousness of faculty a national [and cosmopolitan] orientation, those organizations are increasingly emphasizing the value of the local" (p. 12).

As a classification of institutional (not program or unit) engagement, the classification's framework focuses on three major areas: Foundational Indicators (Institutional Commitment and Institutional Identity and Culture), Curricular Engagement, and Outreach and Partnerships.[2] Following the pilot, the first cycle of classification occurred in 2006, followed by a second round in 2008, and a third in 2010. Following the 2010 cycle, the classification shifted to a 5-year cycle for classification and re-classification, with campuses receiving the classification retaining it for 10 years.[3] The classification was designed to respect the diversity of institutions and their approach to community engagement, honoring an institution's achievements while encouraging a process of inquiry, reflection, and self-assessment as well as ongoing development of programs (Driscoll, 2008). The classification is not designed as a ranking tool but is evaluative in that campuses are either classified or not. There is no hierarchy or levels of classification. Successful campuses are noted publicly by the foundation whereas nothing is released regarding campuses that are not successful with the classification.

Defining *Engagement*

> Community engagement describes the collaboration between institutions of higher education and their larger communities (local, regional/state, national, global) for the mutually beneficial exchange of knowledge and resources in a context of partnership and reciprocity.
>
> The purpose of community engagement is the partnership of college and university knowledge and resources with those of the public and private sectors to enrich scholarship, research, and creative activity; enhance curriculum, teaching and learning; prepare educated, engaged citizens; strengthen democratic values and civic responsibility; address critical societal issues; and contribute to the public good. (Brown University Swearer Center, 2016)

The way in which the Carnegie Foundation defines *community engagement* has two parts: the first focuses on the processes of engagement and the second on the purposes. Central to the standards of the classification is that the partnership relationships between the campus and the community are characterized by collaboration, reciprocity, and mutuality. As defined in the classification, it

> requires going beyond the expert model that often gets in the way of constructive university-community collaboration,. . . calls on faculty to move beyond "outreach,". . . [and] asks scholars to go beyond "service," with its overtones of noblesse oblige. What it emphasizes is genuine *collaboration*: that the learning and teaching be multidirectional and the expertise shared. It represents a basic reconceptualization of . . . community-based work. (O'Meara & Rice, 2005, pp. 27–28)

Framed in this way, community engagement is not an umbrella concept meant to capture any activity associated with civic education, experiential education, or involvement of campuses with local, regional, national, or global communities. These are valuable educational activities, of which some, depending on how they are designed, could be community engaged. Nor is community engagement intended as institutional commitments ranging from investments to procurements, employment, outreach, and economic development. All of these are important activities that can raise the campus's engagement profile, but they are not a substitute for, nor are they synonymous with, academic and scholarly engagement. Further, nonscholarly forms of engagement require little in terms of organizational change and have little impact on the educational experiences of students or the core academic and scholarly work of faculty.

What the Classification for Community Engagement recognizes is relationships between those in the university and those outside the university that are grounded in the qualities of reciprocity, mutual respect, shared authority, and cocreation of goals and outcomes. Such relationships are by their very nature transdisciplinary (knowledge transcending the disciplines and the college or university) and asset based (where the strengths, skills, and knowledges of those in the community are validated and legitimized).

It is important to reiterate that many activities that take place off campus and involve community interactions are important and valuable. Yet the Carnegie Foundation is classifying community engagement, not applied research, public scholarship, internships, economic development, or student volunteerism. It is classifying institutional commitment to activities across the campus that embody the characteristics of engagement and that directly impact the educational experiences of students, the scholarly work of faculty, and/or align with and reinforce both.

The Documentation Framework

The application is constructed as a documentation framework for providing evidence of community engagement and consists of three parts:

1. Foundational Indicators
2. Curricular Engagement
3. Outreach and Partnerships

Foundational Indicators is divided into two sections—Institutional Commitment and Institutional Identity and Culture. The evidence requested in these sections is, as the heading suggests, foundational to institutional community engagement. Under Institutional Identity and Culture, the questions pertain to mission and vision, recognition, assessment and data, marketing materials, and community engagement as a leadership priority. For Institutional Commitment, the questions focus on infrastructure, budget and fund-raising, tracking and documentation, assessment and data, professional development, community voice, faculty recruitment and promotion, student leadership, and the significance of community engagement in the strategic plan of the campus. At the end of the Foundational Indicators section, applicants are instructed to

> review the responses to Foundational Indicators . . . and determine whether community engagement is "institutionalized"—that is, whether all or most of the Foundational Indicators have been documented with specificity. If so, applicants are encouraged to continue with the application. If not, applicants are encouraged to withdraw from the process and apply in the next round. (Brown University Swearer Center, 2016)

The purpose of applying this kind of filter to the process is because the Foundational Indicators are, by definition, *foundational* to the institutionalization of curricular engagement and outreach and partnership activity. For many campuses, reaching this point in the application allows for a reflective pause to assess the campus's engagement portfolio. In each cycle, nearly half of all campuses that request an application do not submit it for review. A survey during the 2015 cycle indicated the primary reason as the realization of unreadiness to submit a successful application. At the same time the framework of the application provides a blueprint for campuses to determine where they have strengths and where they can direct their efforts to improve community engagement across the campus.

The next section, Curricular Engagement, is explained in the framework as "the teaching, learning and scholarship that engages faculty, students, and community in mutually beneficial and respectful collaboration.

Their interactions address community identified needs, deepen students' civic and academic learning, enhance community well-being, and enrich the scholarship of the institution" (Brown University Swearer Center, 2016). The focus is on the extent to which community engagement is part of the central academic experience of the campus, and questions are aimed at the number of students impacted, the breadth of courses offered, the depth of the curriculum, the goals of learning outcomes, and assessment of community engagement outcomes.

The final section, Outreach and Partnerships, is described as

> two different but related approaches to community engagement. The first focuses on the application and provision of institutional resources for community use. The latter focuses on collaborative interactions with community and related scholarship for the mutually beneficial exchange, exploration, and application of knowledge, information, and resources (research, capacity building, economic development, etc.). The distinction between these two centers on the concepts of reciprocity and mutual benefit which are explicitly explored and addressed in partnership activities. (Brown University Swearer Center, 2016)

Outreach questions focus on the programs and institutional resources provided for the community, which, although not considered engagement, are important complements to engagement activities. Partnership questions focus on evidence of mutuality and reciprocity in relationships and ask for examples to be provided in "the partnership grid," which is intended to capture a sense of the institution's depth and breadth of interactive partnerships that demonstrate reciprocity and mutual benefit. Campuses are asked to provide examples that are representative of the range of forms and topical foci of partnerships across a sampling of disciplines and units.

As with any assessment instrument, there are limitations to the documentation framework. As a benchmarking tool, it is largely descriptive, asking for self-reported data/documentation. Unlike an accreditation process, there is no site visit through which to gather evidence that can be triangulated with the documentation provided. Further, for the most part, the documentation framework does not assess the quality of practices; for example, reviewers may know that a certain number of service-learning courses took place in a particular year, but the framework cannot get at the quality of the service-learning in those courses. It also does not assess quality of engagement practices.

Re-Classification

The re-classification documentation framework follows the same structure as the first-time framework. It is designed to allow campuses to gather evidence

TABLE 1.1
The Number of Campuses Classified for Community Engagement

Classification Year	Campuses Classified
2006	74
2008	120
2010	121
2015	83 First-time
	157 Re-classification
	240 Total

of current community engagement commitments and activities, but it also asks for evidence about how community engagement has advanced since the last application. The key to re-classification is the ability to provide evidence of how community engagement has become deeper, more pervasive, better integrated, and increasingly sustained. The focus is on depth and quality within a sustainable institutional context, not greater quantity per se.

As an evidence-based reflective process focusing on what has changed since receiving the classification, the re-classification framework is structured to include narrative responses allowing for explanation of changes that have occurred since the previous classification. The narratives are designed to address (a) what currently exists, (b) changes since the last classification, and (c) relevant supporting evidence.

In addition to evidence provided in the application, the re-classification framework also selectively requests links to relevant campus web resources, unlike the first-time framework. Reviewers may want to examine websites to provide additional clarification of the responses in the application. Reviewers also may ask for a telephone conversation to clarify evidence provided. The re-classification framework provides an opportunity to tell a campus's story of engagement over the long term and to indicate its trajectory for the future, looking ahead to re-classification in another 10 years.

Motivations for Classification

Campuses seek the Carnegie Classification for a number of reasons (for the number of classified campuses, see Table 1.1). The most prevalent is to undergo a structured process of institutional self-assessment and self-study. Putting together an application, gathering evidence and reflecting on it, and understanding areas of strength and weakness of institutional engagement is a way of improving practice and advancing community

Box 1.1

The Benefits of Classification

From the director of the Center for Community Engagement at a classified campus:

> This is one of the highest forms of recognition possible in our field. . . .
> If you are at all interested in a process of self-assessment and quality
> improvement, applying for this Carnegie Classification is a fine way to
> achieve that goal. . . . This opportunity allowed us to lift up elements
> of our institutional mission and distinctiveness that are not necessarily
> represented in the national data on colleges and universities, and it also
> helped us prepare for both re-accreditation and our current strategic
> planning process. (Anonymous, personal communication, 2015)

engagement on campus. The application process is a way to bring the disparate parts of the campus together to advance a unified agenda. At the same time, it allows for the identification of promising practices that can be shared across the institution.

Campuses also seek the classification as a way of legitimizing community engagement work that may not have received public recognition and visibility. Additionally, the classification is used as a way to demonstrate accountability, that the institution is fulfilling its mission to serve the public good. The classification process can also serve as a catalyst for change, fostering institutional alignment for community-based teaching, learning, and scholarship. While fostering all of these processes, the application is further used to crystalize an institutional identity around community engagement. Whether a research university or a community college or a liberal arts institution, a campus may also be community engaged, creating distinction for itself. For example, the University of North Carolina at Greensboro claimed this status following re-classification in 2015, highlighting that it is 1 of only 50 campuses nationally classified by Carnegie for both high research activity and community engagement. Like the University of North Carolina at Greensboro, campuses seek the classification to clarify institutional identity and mission in a way that distinguishes their institutions from peers (see Box 1.1).

Creating an Institutional Culture of Community Engagement

For many if not all campuses, committing to community engagement means undertaking a new set of practices, creating new structures, and revising policies—it is coincident with organizational change. Prior to the establishment of the Carnegie Classification for Community Engagement, Eckel, Hill, and Green (1998) conducted a national study examining institutional change, particularly change that could be considered "transformational." Campuses demonstrating transformational change were exhibiting change that "(1) alters the culture of the institution by changing select underlying assumptions and institutional behaviors, processes, and products; (2) is deep and pervasive, affecting the whole institution; (3) is intentional; and (4) occurs over time" (Eckel et al., 1998, p. 3). Changes that alter "the culture of the institution" are those that require "major shifts in an institution's culture—the common set of beliefs and values that creates a shared interpretation and understanding of events and actions" (Eckel et al., 1998, p. 3).

This attention to deep and pervasive change focuses on the idea that "institution-wide patterns of perceiving, thinking, and feeling; shared understandings; collective assumptions; and common interpretive frameworks are the ingredients of this 'invisible glue' called institutional culture" (Eckel et al., 1998, p. 3). It is precisely these elements of institutional culture that constitute the Foundational Indicators of the community engagement framework.

Eckel and colleagues (1998) concluded that efforts being made in higher education around "connecting institutions to their communities" offered the potential for transformational change. This could occur, they write, because

> these connections can contribute to the reshaping of institutional practices and purposes. . . . They may cause researchers to rethink the types of grants they seek, the ways they disseminate their findings, and the range and types of audiences for their findings. . . . They may reconsider the types of service rewarded through merit pay and promotion and tenure policies, and they may adopt wider definitions of scholarship that include application and integration (Boyer, 1990). . . . Faculty may incorporate service and outreach in their classes and curricula, and students may participate in co-curricular activities (such as internships or service learning) that place them in the community where they can apply their learning to solving real-world problems. (p. 7)

Transformational change occurs when shifts in the institution's culture have developed to the point where they are both pervasive across the institution and deeply embedded in practices throughout the institution (see Figure 1.1).

The construct of deep and pervasive engagement is a useful lens through which to view the Carnegie Community Engagement documentation framework. It is likely that campuses that are in quadrants 1 and 2,

Figure 1.1. Working toward transformational change.

		Depth	
		High	Low
Pervasiveness	Low	Adjustment (1)	Isolated change (2)
	High	Far-reaching change (3)	Transformational change (4)

Source: Adapted from Eckel, Hill, and Green (1998).

based on their community engagement efforts, either do not apply for the classification, begin the process of applying and stop after realizing that there is not enough evidence to satisfy the criteria of the Foundational Indicators, or are not successful with their applications. Campuses that are successful with the classification are able to provide sufficient evidence to demonstrate that they are in quadrant 3 or are somewhere between 3 and 4. These are campuses where community engagement is deep and pervasive, where changes in practices, structures, and policies have created an institutional culture of community engagement.

According to the Eckel and colleagues (1998) model, depth is a key element of transformation, but it is not enough. As they point out, "A deep change is not necessarily broad . . . . It is possible for deep changes to occur within specific units or academic departments without being widespread throughout the institution" (p. 4). There could be a few faculty in a few departments, all doing quality community engagement in their courses and in their research, but if the practice is not widespread across the institution, no organizational transformation is occurring.

Pervasiveness, according to Eckel and colleagues (1998), "refers to the extent to which the change is far-reaching within the institution. The more pervasive the change, the more it crosses unit boundaries and touches different parts of the institution" (p. 4).

One way that the dimension of pervasiveness has been expressed is through institution-wide coordinating infrastructure that facilitates deep community engagement across the campus. These central offices develop depth across the institution, creating and maintaining an inventory of the services, activities, and relationships of its institutional members, identifying and aligning key areas of strength and priority for the university/ college campus, and establishing and evaluating progress toward those priorities. In this role, there is a focus on greater attention toward and ability to track community engagement activities and outcomes across the institution. There is also a focus on intentionality—the intention to be aware of and, to the extent it makes sense in context, to coordinate and collaborate together in areas of shared interest. This includes attention to the role of the center in communicating with and interconnecting faculty, staff, and students both together and with community partners to understand where opportunities exist to coordinate and leverage current or future activities toward complementary and common goals. Robust infrastructure functions in ways that create greater depth and that facilitate deep engagement across the campus to create institutional transformation.

Common Challenges

A letter of congratulations from the Carnegie Foundation informs a campus of success and includes feedback on continuing to advance community engagement on campus. The 2015 letter noted that "even among the most effective applications, there are areas of practice in need of continued development. As a way of improving your institutional practices and to position your campus for successful re-classification in the future," classified campuses were encouraged "to attend to the areas of (1) assessment, (2) reciprocal partnerships, (3) faculty rewards, and (4) integration and alignment with other institutional initiatives." These four areas represent common challenges campuses face as they work to institutionalize community engagement.

Assessment

Applications need to demonstrate systematic assessment of community engagement across a broad range of purposes. Essential for understanding impact and for continuous improvement, assessment is built into the framework throughout—assessing community perceptions of institutional engagement; tracking and recording of institution-wide engagement data; assessment of the impact of community engagement on students, faculty, community, and institution; identification and assessment of student learning outcomes in curricular engagement; and ongoing feedback mechanisms for partnerships.

Reciprocal Partnerships

Partnerships require a high level of understanding of and intentional practices specifically directed to reciprocity and mutuality. Campuses are encouraged to attend to processes of initiating and nurturing collaborative, two-way partnerships and developing strategies for systematic communication. Maintaining authentically collaborative, mutually beneficial partnerships takes ongoing commitment and attention to this critical aspect of community engagement.

Faculty Rewards

With regard to faculty rewards for roles in community engagement, it is difficult to create a campus culture of community engagement when there are not clearly articulated incentives for faculty to prioritize this work. Campuses should provide evidence of clear policies for recognizing community engagement in teaching and learning, and in research and creative activity, along with criteria that validate appropriate methodologies and scholarly artifacts. Campuses are encouraged to initiate study, dialogue, and reflection to promote and reward the scholarship of engagement more fully.

Integration and Alignment With Other Institutional Initiatives

Finally, campuses that are institutionalizing community engagement should consider how community engagement can be integrated with other institutional initiatives. Community engagement offers often-untapped possibilities for alignment with other campus priorities and initiatives to achieve greater impact—for example, first-year programs that include community engagement, learning communities in which community engagement is integrated into the design, or diversity initiatives that explicitly link active and collaborative community-based teaching and learning with the academic success of underrepresented students.

Strategies for Effective Applications

The first-time classification framework is available on the Swearer Center website (Brown University Swearer Center, 2016) with an embedded "guide" for applicants. It is advisable for applicants undertaking the re-classification framework to consult the first-time information from the guide. Because this is an institutional classification, evidence for community engagement often comes from many parts of the campus as well as from community partners. Campuses that have been successful in achieving the classification report that it has been highly beneficial to form a cross-institutional team with community representation to work on the application.

Although it is understandable that applicants will want to tell everything about their campus's community engagement activity, it is necessary to be judicious in selecting the most important and compelling evidence for the application. Each section of the application has word limits.

In constructing an application, look for alignment across the sections of the application and analyze whether the evidence triangulates (e.g., if the president's statements say that community engagement is a strategic priority but the question about the strategic plan does not indicate community engagement as a strategic priority, there is not alignment). Also, tell the whole story: An authentic understanding of community engagement is enhanced when a campus describes successes as well as activities that didn't go as planned. The latter provide opportunities for learning and improvement and can be described accordingly.

When crafting an application, it is important to convey a coherent narrative. Also, don't leave blanks. If there is no evidence for a particular area, explain why and what you are doing about it. Finally, it is important to keep in mind that campuses are classified for engagement that has been implemented, not aspired to. Many applications provide answers about what the campus will do or what the parties plan to accomplish. These may be important activities and directions, but the classification is seeking evidence of implementation.

Leveraging the Classification

We encourage campuses to not just earn the classification but to use it to further advance their efforts and to also envision a 10-year plan that will sustain, deepen, and expand community engagement, providing evidence for re-classification. As one example of using the classification, a campus reported that "the classification has been leveraged to great results in four ways:

1. First, the information compiled for our application greatly assisted us in preparing the university's documentation related to engagement for our

Southern Association of Colleges and Schools reaffirmation presentation the following year. The receipt of the Carnegie designation itself
provided de facto evidence that the university was continually assessing
and improving its engagement enterprise.

2. Second, the Carnegie designation provided the framework for development of engagement priorities in the new university strategic plan last
year.

3. Third, we have incorporated the Carnegie classification, and models of
engagement at fellow Carnegie CE [Community Engagement] institutions into our faculty development programs. The classification has also
provided an impetus to reexamine and improve our faculty engagement .
grants and other related programs.

4. Finally, the Carnegie CE classification has provided the university
with a branding opportunity. We have seen much more promotion of
our engagement programs and overall outreach mission by the central administration and marketing department since receipt of the CE
(Anonymous, personal communication, 2015).

A common refrain is that the most valuable part of the classification
is the process of self-study, which is why the foundation encourages campuses to participate in the classification process even if they are unsure
as to whether they have enough evidence to be successful. If unsuccessful, the campus will have brought together a range of stakeholders for
common conversation and self-assessment and used the documentation
framework as a blueprint for constructing an institutional architecture of
engagement on the campus. Unsuccessful campuses are offered opportunities for specific feedback following the review process. Many campuses that go through the process and are unsuccessful learn from the
process and get feedback, returning in the next cycle with a successful
application.

For campuses that are successful, use the classification to make the
most of your success. Use the classification process and the data gathered
for the application to strategically plan for advancing the community
engagement work of the campus, envisioning where the campus will be in
10 years having furthered an institutional culture of engagement—creating
a narrative that can be told through an application for re-classification.

Notes

1. For example, service-learning, community service, public service, engaged
scholarship, and so on.

2. In 2006 and 2008, the process allowed for campuses to classify under Curricular Engagement, Outreach and Partnerships, or both. By the 2010 cycle, there

was no longer a choice of areas—to be classified as a community engaged campus, evidence had to be provided in both areas.

3. In 2009, the administration of the classification was hosted at the New England Resource Center for Higher Education at the University of Massachusetts, Boston. In 2017, the host site of the classification moved to the Swearer Center at Brown University.

References

Boyer, E. L. (1990). *Scholarship reconsidered: Priorities of the professoriate.* Lawrenceville, NJ: Princeton University Press.

Brown University Swearer Center. (2016). *Carnegie Classification frameworks.* Retrieved from https://www.brown.edu/academics/college/swearer/carnegie-community-engagement-classification

Campus Compact. (1999). *Presidents' declaration on the civic responsibility of higher education.* Providence, RI: Author. Retrieved from https://kdpol43vw6z2dl-w631ififc5-wpengine.netdna-ssl.com/wp-content/uploads/2009/02/Presidents-Declaration.pdf

Driscoll, A. (2008, January–February) Carnegie's community-engagement classification: Intentions and insights. *Change, 40*(1), 38–41.

Eckel, P., Hill, B., & Green, M. (1998). *On change: En route to transformation* (Occasional Paper No. 120, Series of the ACE Project on Leadership and Institutional Transformation). Washington DC, American Council for Education.

Furco, A. (1999). *Self-assessment rubric for the institutionalization of service-learning in higher education.* Retrieved from https://digitalcommons.unomaha.edu/slceslgen/127/

Holland, B. A. (2000, Fall). Institutional impacts and organizational issues related to service-learning [Special Issue]. *Michigan Journal of Community Service Learning*, pp. 52–60.

Hollander, E., Saltmarsh, J., & Zlotkowski, E. (2001). Indicators of engagement. In M. E. Kenny, L. A. K. Simon, K. Kiley-Brabeck, & R. M. Lerner (Eds.), *Learning to serve: Promoting civil society through service learning* (pp. 31–49). Outreach Scholarship Series, Vol. 7. Boston, MA: Kluwer.

Kecskes, K., & Muyllaert, J. (1997). *Benchmark worksheet for the Western Region Campus Compact Consortium Grants Program.* Bellingham, WA: Western Washington University.

McCormick, A. C., & Zhao, C. M. (2005). Rethinking and reframing the Carnegie classification. *Change: The Magazine of Higher Learning, 37*(5), 51–57.

O'Meara, K. A., & Rice, R. E. (Eds.). (2005). *Faculty priorities reconsidered: Encouraging multiple forms of scholarship.* San Francisco, CA: Jossey-Bass.

Rhoades, G. (2009). Carnegie, DuPont circle, and the AAUP: (Re)shaping a cosmopolitan, locally engaged professoriate. *Change: The Magazine of Higher Learning, 41*(1), 8–15.

PART ONE

FIRST-TIME CLASSIFICATION

Chapter Two

FOUNDATIONAL INDICATORS

Lina D. Dostilio

Introduction

Ten years ago, I prepared a memo to my then provost recommending that Duquesne University pursue the 2008 Carnegie Classification for Community Engagement. The rationale was that securing the classification would

> publicly confirm that Duquesne actively pursues its mission and aspects of its institutional strategic plan, would differentiate it from other universities in the region with which we compete for regional student enrollment, and would lead to more systematized communication and collaboration among community engagement efforts across the University. (Dostilio, 2007)

It did these things, but the institutional self-reflection and data collection exercise required to secure the classification in 2008 (and then again in 2015) also helped us to realize something greater: It was perhaps the single most significant step Duquesne had taken in broadly institutionalizing community engagement.

During our first-time classification, I was the director of service-learning at Duquesne and responsible for the university's largest community engagement program—a service-learning course requirement for every undergraduate, embedded in existing credit-bearing disciplinary classes across the majors. In 2007, Duquesne enrolled an average of 5,300 undergraduates across its 11 schools. Duquesne University is a Spiritan Catholic institution, animated, at that time, by a literal commitment to its mission of "service to the Church, the community, the nation and the world" (Duquesne University Mission Statement, n.d.). The student volunteerism program also involved a large percentage of the undergraduate student body. Although I understood the classification to emphasize a holistic framework for community engagement, I felt the strength of our student community engagement efforts and their associated community partnerships were likely to qualify us for the classification. Even so, the likelihood of earning the classification was not my primary motivation to pursue it. I felt the process of assembling our application and the ways it would involve our institutional leadership was exactly what Duquesne needed to spur the next phase of its commitment to community engagement. We used the classification as a tool to educate the university and facilitate reflection on the importance of community-engaged scholarship, institutional-community partnerships, and sustained institutionalization (beyond student involvement). Five years after our initial classification, we (Dostilio & Getkin, 2013) wrote the following:

> The processes used to secure the Carnegie Classification for Community Engagement elevated the conversation about engagement [at Duquesne] beyond service-learning and volunteerism. It challenged campus stakeholders to think about greater goals for engagement than simply implementing service-learning. Campus consciousness began to focus on deeper levels of engagement. (p. 152)

And so I proposed that we apply. Within that initial memo to the provost, I estimated that it would take us a year to assemble our documentation and explained that it would require (a) university-wide evidence collection involving the many stakeholders within the community engagement effort, (b) a centrally coordinated process that leveraged a graduate student assistant who had just concluded a term supporting the university's decennial institutional accreditation, and (c) executive endorsement, saying, "It is important that the entire Carnegie Engagement Classification process be endorsed by the executive office as supporting the university's mission and the mission's promotion." Our administration agreed to pursue the classification, and I became our project lead.

In the 2008 application framework, the Foundational Indicators included the two sections described in chapter 1 plus an optional section. The first required section on Institutional Identity and Culture asked questions about how community engagement was included in the institution's mission or vision statement, its recognition in awards and celebration, the system for assessing community perceptions about the effectiveness of engagement with the community and how the resulting data are used, and how it is emphasized in marketing materials. The second required section on Institutional Commitment included questions about how community engagement is promoted and advanced through the executive leadership's communications, the existence of coordinating infrastructure and internal budgetary support, the dedication of external funding and other fundraising, systematic campus-wide assessment and evaluation mechanisms, the use of the resulting data to improve courses and other engagement efforts, inclusion in the institution's strategic plan, professional development to support faculty and staff engaging with the community, and the community's voice or role in planning for community engagement. There was an optional set of questions in the 2008 classification that included questions about search and recruitment policies encouraging the hiring of community-engaged faculty, students having leadership in community engagement, promotion and tenure policies rewarding engaged scholarship, and inclusion of community engagement on student transcripts (these questions are no longer optional—they are required).

Positioning Our Application as a Self-Study

Community engagement was very decentralized at Duquesne. Student involvement in community-based experiences was facilitated by the service-learning program, student volunteerism office, and Campus Ministry center, but there was no coordination among these units. Beyond these, there was a proliferation of initiatives and centers throughout the schools that supported various kinds of community involvement, again with little cross-effort collaboration. Like many first-time applicants, we felt worthy of the classification but did not have our work organized and documented in a way that easily facilitated our application. Our first task was to develop a comprehensive understanding of what initiatives existed to determine which fit the Carnegie definition of community engagement, how they assessed the various impacts of their engagement, and what partnerships might be included in our list of 10 to 15 exemplars.

We were just wrapping up our institutional reaccreditation and felt that using the language of "self-study" rather than "application" would better characterize the process as institutional self-reflection. At that time on our campus, external accolades were less motivating to faculty and staff than processes that brought institutional growth and change. External endorsements are powerful motivators for institutional leaders, but faculty and staff who are seeking to influence institutional support for matters important to them find self-studies more promising. Additionally, our faculty respected the notion of self-study as it is a mainstay of the academic program review process and is associated with rigorous, systematic data collection used to improve a degree program, unit, or school. In this case, we felt that organizing a "self-study" of our community engagement initiatives and the institution's support for them would better convey our intent and approach.

The provost presented the classification and our plans for a self-study to the President's Cabinet and we presented the same information to the Council of Deans. We asked the deans of each school and cabinet members (which included the vice president of student life and the vice president of business engagement) to forward the names of faculty and staff who were working on community engagement initiatives. We invited those named to two open forums where we discussed the Carnegie Classification, the definition of *community engagement* advanced therein, and the goals of our application—namely, to deepen institutional support for community engagement and to institutionalize our practices through our efforts. At the same time, we were assembling a catalog of institutional documents that provided evidence of the nature and breadth of community engagement at Duquesne.

Getting Our Arms Around It All

We considered those invited to the open forums to be community-engaged stakeholders and we circulated a survey asking them to describe the ways they engaged the community and their methods to assess the work's impact on community, faculty, and students; we also asked them to suggest additional community-engaged stakeholders or community partners who might be contacted for information as well as review the catalog of source documents and contribute additional documents from their schools and units; and last, we asked them to nominate a partnership that should be included in our 10 to 15 exemplars. We also included 2 additional questions, meant to aid the process, that we didn't anticipate being used as documentation within our application. We asked respondents to describe how they felt the classification would benefit their units or schools and for permission to quote them about these benefits in our self-study promotional materials, and we also asked what concerns they had about the process.

To this point, I partnered with a graduate assistant and our associate provost to work on the process. We began to hold update meetings with the leader of our student volunteerism office, our chief financial officer (CFO), who was very active in community affairs, and the leader of our University-Community Collaborative project, which was an outgrowth of our Housing and Urban Development–funded Community Outreach Partnership Center.

From the initial round of surveys (43) we sent out an additional 21 surveys. In total, we had about 58 completed surveys that informed our data collection. We used a few of the initial respondents' perceptions of the self-study's benefits in campus news stories about the process and on a website we created. Our intent was to well-publicize the self-study, both as a way to attract and include all community-engaged stakeholders but also to communicate the importance of community engagement at Duquesne. Within the surveys, we had been referred to 23 community partners who our campus stakeholders felt would be strong informants on Duquesne's community engagement efforts. The surveys also listed about 24 programs or initiatives that were repeatedly referenced as emblematic of community engagement as characterized in the classification. We set up a protocol and asked the 23 community partners and representatives of the 24 exemplar programs to participate in an interview. Our graduate assistant conducted a total of 38 interviews with community and campus stakeholders. These interviews provided more descriptive information about partnerships, assessment, facilitators, and barriers and secured the buy-in and support of our most engaged faculty, staff, and community partners for the self-study and also for the institutionalization of community engagement more broadly.

With the additional documents submitted by our community-engaged stakeholders, our archive contained 139 documents that provided evidence of Duquesne's commitments to community engagement. These ranged from press releases to web pages, from university publications such as magazines and newspapers to speeches and institutional documents such as the core curriculum, strategic plan, and faculty handbook.

We were awash in data. In sum, we had 58 surveys, 38 interviews, and 139 documents. For a campus whose community engagement efforts were decentralized and not yet institutionalized, this sort of data collection was paramount to (a) documenting the rich range of community engagement activities, (b) discovering the ways in which stakeholders spoke of their work and how different characterizations of community engagement pointed to different intentions and purposes for community engagement, (c) identifying which units and schools were particularly oriented toward community engagement, and (d) gathering the diversity of ways community engagement was assessed and how the results were used. Having a comprehensive data collection strategy also generated feelings of inclusion;

many stakeholders felt their work mattered to the self-study and, in turn, that community engagement mattered to Duquesne.

Answering Each Question

We used the questions on the classification application framework as our organizing schema. Each question had its own tab in a spreadsheet, and for each question, we assembled excerpts from the surveys, documents, and interviews. Our graduate assistant, Deirdre Assenza, was paramount to this process. Immersed in our data 20 hours a week, she embraced the rigorous and systematic approach we were seeking, and her professional experience as a librarian translated to impeccable data organization and recall skills.

We found the questions about mission, awards, marketing materials, strategic plans, professional development opportunities, and how leadership promotes community engagement easily answered by consulting our data. The questions about assessment, funding, and promotion and tenure were more difficult.

At that time, Duquesne had no institution-wide systematic approach to assess community perceptions of its engagement or the impact of engagement on faculty, students, community, or the institution. We did, however, have many diverse examples of how this was done at the unit or initiative level. We chose to thematically present the existing assessment strategies, realizing that this might fall short of what was expected for the classification. We organized and presented the strategies for assessing community perceptions of Duquesne's engagement across programs in four buckets: (a) formal assessment strategies, (b) informal community participant feedback, (c) informal assessment strategies using student work, and (d) formal assessment rubrics; we then gave examples of each, sometimes listing as many as 10 different programs' approaches.

With regard to how these data were used, we again pointed to decentralized practices but provided evidence of use. We explained how individual programs employed data for program improvement, documented the various university reports that publicly disseminated the university's community and economic impact, and described how data were used to assemble Duquesne's applications to the President's Community Service Honor Roll, annual Campus Compact membership survey, and Middle States Accreditation Self Study. We readily admitted that there were three different campus systems for tracking and documenting community engagement, including annual reports from the Office of Service-Learning,

Student Volunteerism Office, and Public Affairs community and economic impact reports.

We had evidence to document student, community, and institutional impact assessment and how the results were used, though again, in decentralized ways. I think our approach to the question about assessing impact on faculty is particularly emblematic of our approach overall. We pointed to a number of assessment strategies ranging from interviews with tenured faculty, insights gleaned from course minigrant applications, and evidence of community-engaged scholarship within the annual faculty scholarship catalog. We surmised that faculty did not feel that value for community-engaged scholarship was explicit or consistent, and that led to the provost issuing a statement in support of service-learning as a valued part of teaching. We included this finding and resulting "change" to campus practice, knowing that it fell short of best practices. The provost's statement did not acknowledge the fullness of community-engaged scholarship, nor was it an official change to review, promotion, and tenure policy. However, our intention throughout the self-study process was to be unerringly forthcoming because we felt it would motivate further institutional change by making our opportunities and shortcomings visible. We experienced the same challenges in the questions related to promotion and tenure policies. We chose to answer straightforwardly: Duquesne has a traditional tripartite reward structure of teaching, research, and service. Community-engaged scholarship could be included within one's teaching and research categories, but no specific weight or characterization is given to it. We also admitted that there were no formal plans to revise the institution's tenure and promotion policies. I'm delighted to say this has recently changed, in part because of our choice to approach these questions in both the 2008 and 2015 classifications without any "spin" and because we received feedback on our 2015 application that if the university did not address this gap in review, promotion, and tenure policies that we would not be reclassified in 2025.

The questions about funding also proved to be challenging. During our self-study process, the seniormost member of our team (the associate provost) took a new position. She had the greatest familiarity with our institution's budgetary practices. Though we had reached out to our contributing campus stakeholders to ask them what levels of internal and external funding supported their work, we were not having much luck getting comprehensive answers from the budget and planning office, in part because they had no way of distinguishing generic outreach work from the kind of community engagement included in the classification. With the arrival of a new associate provost who was particularly versed in institutional operations and financial administration, we quickly asked the right questions, and it was recommended that we use the totals Duquesne listed for Public Service in the Integrated Postsecondary Education Data System (IPEDS) as a way to capture the total of external funding dedicated to community engagement.

Closing the Loop

After assembling the application, we summarized our own insights and findings and packaged those as an executive summary:

> Regardless of the outcome of our application to the Carnegie Foundation, the value in this self-study lies within the changes that will come as a result of our own institutional commitments to deepening community engagement at Duquesne. To this end, we make the following recommendations: A) Develop means to systematically assess community *perceptions* of the institution's engagement and the *impact* of engagement activities on the community. B) Emphasize the role of community engagement in search and recruitment policies of faculty and administrators. C) Align institutional policies of promotion and tenure to the importance placed on the integration of community engagement with teaching and research. D) Promote opportunities for departments that specialize in community engagement . . . to meet with one another and share information. E) Support and encourage faculty scholarship that draws upon community engagement. (Dostilio, 2008)

The executive summary, internal recommendations, and full application were presented to the President's Cabinet, the Council of Deans, and to our contributing stakeholders. We also held a celebratory breakfast to thank stakeholders for their investments and contributions, at which we discussed the internal recommendations.

Ripple Effects

Our efforts to take on a rigorous, systematic self-study that anticipated institutional change yielded the results we sought. There were a number of ripple effects, including administrative recognition and support for a more comprehensive set of community-engaged activities, a shift from valuing undirectional service to a more nuanced understanding of community engagement, and an evolution toward institutionalization of community engagement.

Many of Duquesne's answers to the questions that were concerned with institutional strategies, assessment, and support relied on the work being done through the service-learning program. This was because it was the only community engagement effort that was administrated and supported institution-wide. Yet the diversity and strength of community engagement initiatives throughout the schools and units was impressive. It highlighted the need to institutionally support, promote, and recognize a much wider diversity of community-engaged work, including community-engaged research, economic development partnerships, and political and advocacy activities.

Duquesne's mission commitment has been enriched in the 10 years since the classification, in part because of enhanced institutional reflection on the emphasis on reciprocity and mutuality within community engagement and in part because of the Division of Mission and Identity's efforts to amplify the institution's identity as the compass by which its mission is realized. There is now a three-part articulation of the institution's Spiritan Catholic identity that is integrated with its commitments to community engagement: (a) living open to the spirit (sometimes articulated as living open to new perspectives), (b) committing to authentic relationships, and (c) walking with those on the margins (Weaver, Dostilio, & DiMaggio, in press). What was once a focus on unidirectional service activities has become a far more reciprocal and sustainable approach done in the context of partnerships.

Finally, Duquesne has embraced an understanding and institutionalization of community engagement that is reflective of the definition and practices advanced in the Carnegie Classification. In the 2003–2008 strategic plan, the reference to engagement was student focused and stated that "opportunities for leadership and service will be expanded" (Duquesne University, 2003). In the 2010–2015 plan, the commitment to service reached across the institution's functions and commitments and was phrased as one of 10 priority goals: "Service to others will be an essential theme in all of our efforts" (Duquesne University, 2008). The university is in the process of another strategic planning period, and community engagement is one of three central themes, characterized through mutuality, partnerships, and sustained engagement over time. The university is also creating a senior engagement officer position to better coordinate the institutionalization of community engagement moving forward.

I have since moved on from Duquesne University, taking the assistant vice chancellor of community engagement position at the University of Pittsburgh (Pitt). Pitt is a premier urban research institution that is also considering applying for the classification. Once again, I will be in the role of stewarding a first-time applicant. Knowing that the classification has the potential to catalyze and accelerate the adoption of best practices and a unified concept of community engagement is a powerful motivator to recommend pursuing it in this new institutional context.

References

Dostilio, L. D. (2007, September). *Carnegie Classification briefing memo.* Unpublished memorandum, Duquesne University, Pittsburgh, Pennsylvania.

Dostilio, L. D. (2008, September). *Executive summary.* Unpublished report, Duquesne University, Pittsburgh, Pennsylvania.

Dostilio, L. D., & Getkin, D. (2013). Service-learning as catalyst for integrating community engagement across core academic functions. In J. Jacob, S. Sutin, J. Weidman, & J. Yeager (Eds.), *Community engagement in higher education: Policy reforms and practice* (pp. 139–169). Boston, MA: Sense Publishers.

Duquesne University. (2003). *2003–2008 strategic plan.* Pittsburgh, PA: Author.

Duquesne University. (2010). *2010–2015 strategic plan.* Pittsburgh, PA: Author.

Duquesne University Mission Statement. (n.d.). Retrieved from http://www .duq.edu/about/mission-and-identity/mission-statement

Weaver, D., Dostilio, L. D., & DiMaggio, L. J. (forthcoming). The difference charism makes to civically-focused community engagement: Curricular and co-curricular reflections. *Engaging Pedagogies in Catholic Higher Education, 4*(1).

Chapter Three

CURRICULAR ENGAGEMENT

What the Community Engagement Classification Taught Me

John Reiff

Introduction

When the Carnegie Foundation for the Advancement of Teaching announced the opportunity to apply for the first round of institutions receiving the Elective Classification for Community Engagement in 2006, I thought this was a perfect opportunity for my institution, the University of Massachusetts Amherst (UMass Amherst), to receive recognition for our work in community engagement. As a land-grant university, UMass had been involved in programs of research and service across the state since its founding.

Since at least the 1960s, faculty had been building community engagement into courses here and there across the campus. In 1994, a visionary faculty member (David Schimmel) had persuaded the provost to establish a funding line for Service-Learning Faculty Fellowships; in turn, the provost had persuaded Dave to chair a Provost's Special Committee on Service-Learning (PCSL) that each year would recruit

10 to 12 faculty to meet monthly for a year, studying the pedagogy and helping each other think through how to redesign their courses to build service-learning into them. In 1999, Dave and one of the first faculty fellows, Art Keene, had captured another line of funding to create an Office of Community Service Learning (OCSL), which was based in Commonwealth Honors College and served the entire campus, and I had been hired in 2000 as the university's first full-time director of service-learning. We were continuing to run the Faculty Fellows Program, adding new service-learning courses across the campus each year, and we had built multicourse programs that were the subject of national service learning scholarship in anthropology, the UMass Alliance for Community Transformation (UACT), which drew upon students as colleagues to facilitate a five-credit service-learning course, and in the Commonwealth Honors College, a yearlong residential academic program for first-year students (Impact) and a two-year program, the Citizen Scholars Program, that culminated in service-learning courses satisfying the honors thesis/project requirement.

Yes, it seemed like UMass Amherst would be a natural for this classification. Then I got the guidance for applying.

If I made the application for the university, I would have to start out by providing a set of "Foundational Indicators." If I could answer yes to all of those questions, then I could go on to fill out the rest of the application. One of the questions asked for a statement from the president or chancellor detailing his or her support for community engagement as a priority of the institution.

I thought, "Before I came to UMass, Chancellor David Scott had asked the Provost's Committee on Service-Learning to run a Chancellor's Community Service Luncheon at the end of every spring and provided funding to invite several hundred community members, students, and faculty—including the students and community agency staff who were receiving awards for outstanding engagement in these campus/community partnerships." After I was hired, I took over managing this event for the provost's committee and heard the chancellor speak forcefully at this annual event about the importance of UMass students and faculty engaging with the communities around the campus. He could write a great statement articulating the value of community engagement to the university and the value of that engagement to the communities around us. He could even quote from the article he had coauthored about our work, "Filling in the Moat Around the Ivory Tower," for a book titled *Learning to Serve: Promoting Civil Society Through Service Learning* (Miller & Scott, 2002).

However, chancellors don't stay forever, and David Scott retired. When a new chancellor was appointed, I organized the Chancellor's Community Service Luncheon for the new chancellor. He attended and spoke, then sent word to me that he wanted the event to be discontinued. Looking at the Carnegie application, I thought about all the public statements I had heard from this chancellor; they were all about either the importance of faculty research and the role of that research in raising the university's standings in the rankings of research universities, or about the value of "new dirt"—the disruption caused by adding multiple new buildings to the campus infrastructure. Since his appointment, my colleagues and I had continued our work with community engagement as a niche enterprise in a complex and decentralized organization, largely outside his attention and outside his stated priorities. I couldn't imagine him writing the kind of statement the application would need, so I didn't pursue the application. The Community Engagement Classification had taught me its first lesson:

Lesson 1: Secure active involvement from upper-level administrators (the chancellor or president and provost, who are responsible for taking an institution-wide view) if you seek to move from a niche enterprise to an institutional initiative or commitment.

Without that involvement, I dropped the idea of applying.

But I thought again: chancellors don't stay forever. Perhaps the next chancellor will place more value on community engagement, and we can apply in the next round. That was exactly what happened.

First Application for the Classification

The next chancellor, Thomas W. Cole Jr., came to UMass in 2007 out of retirement from a career that included serving as the first president of Clark Atlanta University, a historically Black institution. His early public talks made clear that he saw higher educational institutions as important resources for their local communities, so it was logical to approach him as a supporter for the application. At the same time, Vice Provost for Outreach Sharon Fross (who oversaw a range of outward-facing programs, including extension services; the campus radio station; continuing and professional education; and the University Without Walls, a degree-completion program for working adults) suggested that we apply for the classification, offering a critical resource by assigning a staff member,

Bill Miller, to oversee the process. Fross organized a planning committee that included the deputy provost, the associate provost for academic
planning and assessment, staff from the library and the office of the vice
chancellor for research, two faculty members with significant community
partnerships, herself, Miller, and me.

*Lesson 2: Bringing together perspectives from a broad range of the units and
roles in a complex decentralized university was a key early decision allowing
us to identify multiple forms of community engagement and a range of policies and programs.*

In the 2008 round of applications, institutions could choose to be classified on the basis of curricular engagement, community partnerships,
or both. We decided to go for both, with Miller overseeing collection of
data about community partnerships through the extension office, faculty
research, and other programs, while I collected data on curricular engagement, primarily service-learning, and the community partnerships underlying curricular engagement. During the final stages of data collection and
writing, I was able to hire a graduate student, Koni Denham, to assist with
gathering and presenting data on service-learning.

*Lesson 3: Having staff (in our case, Miller, Denham, and myself) who are
familiar with community engagement and can dedicate the time to collect,
analyze, and write up the data on the institution's work in this field is critical.*

Curricular Engagement: Three Challenges

As we began collecting data to answer the questions on Curricular
Engagement, we ran into three challenges. Which courses should we
count? Who in the community will partner with our service-learning
courses? What instruments will best measure student learning outcomes,
and how should we use those assessments?

Courses

Over the past 20 years, UMass Amherst has had three ways of answering
the question regarding courses. In the mid-1990s, the internship office in
student affairs, working in collaboration with the PCSL, created a list of
service-learning courses identified by members of the PCSL. Each year

thereafter 10 to 12 courses offered by the most recent cohort of service-learning faculty fellows would be added to the list. When I was hired as director of OCSL in 2000, OCSL took responsibility for the list, which contained around 100 courses, and we began adding 10 to 12 courses per year. Then I began hearing from students that in some courses on our list, the faculty member had dropped the service-learning component and, in others, a different faculty member was teaching the course with no awareness that the course had once had service-learning as part of it.

We decided that instead of simply adding to the list each year, we'd start each year at zero and list only the courses we could confirm as actually using a service-learning design. In addition to the courses offered through OCSL itself, we e-mailed all the faculty on our previous list and asked if their courses could meet the following five criteria for community service-learning (CSL):

1. Involves students in substantive, ongoing community service activity that is directly integrated into the curriculum in a significant way
2. Develops the service component cooperatively with community partners so that it meets needs identified by the community
3. Prepares students for their work in the community
4. Requires systematic and regular reflection, reporting, and assessment of the service experience—both with faculty and with other students (e.g., reading assignments, oral presentations, journal or final paper submissions that synthesize the service experience)
5. Assesses the impact of the CSL component

When we instituted this new procedure, our annual total dropped from well over 100 to around 40 courses—leaving out, we were convinced, an unknown number of courses that should be counted but whose instructors had not replied to our queries. We realized that we had switched from the problem of overcounting to the problem of undercounting—without solid data on how large either of those problems was.

It was at this point that we began working on the Carnegie Classification application. Denham's work was critical here: she e-mailed, called, and sometimes visited faculty who had once appeared on our list but had dropped from it, eventually confirming that for the most recent academic year, our list of courses should total 103.

After completing the Carnegie application, knowing that we couldn't each year dedicate the staff time to the process that Denham used, we began working to devise a third system for course designation. We asked the Academic Matters Council of the Faculty Senate for approval to designate courses as either service-learning or civic engagement in the registrar's database, rather than simply producing our own lists each semester. Our request sat in line on the Academic Matters Council's agenda for about a year; then a new chair was appointed, who told us that in her view, the council's approval wasn't necessary for a request like ours and we should simply work out a procedure with the registrar. The registrar was happy to add these two course designations to a short list of other searchable course attributes, using a list we would provide each semester before preregistration. We decided that we would ask faculty to answer a few online questions and to upload the most recent syllabus; a subcommittee of the PCSL would review the requests for designation, and designations would be approved for a period of five years (unless the faculty member was no longer using community engagement in the course). This struck a middle ground between the first two approaches to course identification, and given that the identification was part of the registrar's public course listing, we hoped that faculty would feel more incentive to list courses and more obligation to let us know when courses should be removed from the list.

This third process also addressed another problem—quality control. Since the beginning of listing service-learning courses in the 1990s, the PCSL had taken a "big tent" approach: invite faculty to tell us if they are teaching a service-learning course and list it if they say they are. That seemed appropriate, politically, in the early stages of curricular reform, when an underlying goal was to get as many faculty involved as possible. But over time, we began to hear about courses whose faculty proclaimed they were doing service-learning but the courses did not sufficiently prepare students for community engagement or did not involve them in any significant reflection on the experience—or, for that matter, did not organize the community engagement with much input from the organization with which students would be working. By having a faculty committee review a syllabus and a set of answers to key questions (e.g., paralleling the process of assigning general education designations), we could have confidence that courses being listed all met the same minimum thresholds. And if a course failed to meet one of the core criteria, OCSL staff could consult with the faculty member and offer to help revise the course to fulfill all the criteria.

Lesson 4: Institutionalize the designation of service-learning courses by getting them into the registrar's course database.

Community Organizations Partnering With Our Service-Learning Courses

When we started working on the Carnegie Classification application, we knew a great deal about the community partners for the courses run directly out of the OCSL. We also had access to information about community partners for the other signature programs of the campus and for the courses offered by recent participants in the Faculty Fellows Program. But because the majority of service-learning courses were offered by faculty from across the university and because we were unsure about many such courses (as previously discussed), we faced a major information gap about community partnerships.

There was no centralized database for other kinds of community partnerships, either. In the 1990s, the associate chancellor for outreach had a large map on a piece of posterboard in his office with pins on it for all the community partnerships, but that information had disappeared with the passage of time and changes in administrators. So, for this application, as Denham was collecting partnership data from the service-learning faculty she contacted, Miller was doing the same for all the noncurricular programs he was exploring. As we approached the end of writing the application, one of our recommendations to the university was that it create a system for maintaining, sharing, and updating the data we had collected, so when time came for the renewal application to Carnegie (or when any other need arose for information on community partnerships), the data would be current and available.

Lesson 5: Arrange for the creation and maintenance of a community partnership database.

Assessment of Student Learning Outcomes

Assessment was both one of our hardest challenges and one of our easiest sections to write—hard because although OCSL identified learning outcomes for service-learning generally for the campus (academic, personal, and civic learning, with examples of each) and we were able to find half a dozen programs that identified desired learning outcomes more specifically for their own students, we could only find one program—the Citizen Scholars Program, OCSL's own signature program—that assessed learning outcomes and then used that assessment to fine-tune the curriculum (see Reiff & Keene, 2012). Given the paucity of our data, the actual writing was easy; although the four questions about learning outcomes allowed up to

200 words for each question, we took only 67 words to describe how outcomes were assessed and only 38 to describe how assessment results were used in our one program.

Like the absence of a database for community partnerships, the absence of systematic campus-wide assessment of student learning outcomes struck us as a major gap in our programs—one that we should figure out how to fill.

Lesson 6: Engage service-learning faculty from across the campus in identifying desired student learning outcomes, assessing the extent to which and the ways in which students demonstrate those outcomes, and using the assessment data to fine-tune (or overhaul) their courses.

What happened with these gaps is discussed in the following section.

After the Application Was Submitted

After we submitted our application in 2008, a new chancellor arrived, and the national economic disaster began to unfold. (We don't believe there is a causal relationship among these three events—but the second and third drove how we managed the lessons we learned from the application process.) We thought the associate provost for outreach would be a logical person to hold and maintain the community partnership database we had created; however, the new chancellor reorganized his administration and eliminated her position, parceling out the units under her to other preexisting structures. We thought that OCSL could design assessment protocols for student learning outcomes and roll them out to the campus, beginning with the next cohort of service-learning faculty fellows; instead, managing budget cuts in response to economic-crisis-driven reductions in state funding, the campus administration decided to cut OCSL into 2 parts—leaving me in the honors college with a reduced budget and establishing a new service-learning office under the provost, staffed by a 29% lecturer and a 10-hour-per-week graduate assistant. So, as UMass Amherst was receiving the 2008 Carnegie Classification for Community Engagement, instead of moving forward addressing the lessons we had learned through the application process, we were thrown into a struggle simply to keep service-learning and community engagement alive at the university.

Lesson 7: Expect changes in strategy to be driven by changes in circumstances, especially changes in administration.

Soon, changes in administration again brought changes in strategy. In 2011, two years after OCSL had been divided into two units, a new provost asked why there were two units supporting service-learning at UMass, with the bigger one serving only the honors college and the smaller one serving the entire campus. He engineered the recombination of the two units into one, but this time operating out of his office. To indicate our new organizational position, we took on a new name, claiming civic engagement as part of our mission: UMass Office of Civic Engagement and Service-Learning (CESL).

One other element shifted in a significant way after we received our initial Community Engagement Classification. Our signature program, the Citizen Scholars Program, had grown over time from two to four courses taken in sequence, with the capstone course modeled after the course on organizing taught by Marshall Ganz at Harvard University. When Mary Hannah Henderson, the graduate student who had brought us her version of Ganz's course, told us that she was teaching it for the last time because she needed to write her dissertation, I thought I should sit in on it in case it fell to me to teach it in the future. Henderson told me that if we were meeting periodically to discuss what was happening in the course, it would work better if we each took on our own organizing projects, so we could apply the lessons of the course to our own projects (and use the projects to illuminate the lessons of the course). She asked me to figure out a purpose statement for my project: *I am organizing [whom] to [do what]*. I decided to frame my job as my organizing project: *I am organizing the faculty and administration of UMass Amherst to embrace and support service-learning and civic engagement.* I never ended up teaching the course, but viewing my job through an organizer's lens for a semester changed me and the way I understood my work; yes, I was a faculty member and an administrator, but in my own internal job description, I was first of all an organizer. This framework shaped my approach to renewing our Carnegie Classification in 2015: given that the criteria for classification were announced long in advance of the submission deadline, how might I organize faculty and administrators to build a stronger case for the application by developing structures that better match the criteria?

Conclusion

Looking back on this history, I have come to see the Carnegie Community Engagement Classification as a recognition not of accomplishment (yes! our institution is community-engaged!) but of process (our institution has enough people in enough different roles and enough structures and policies in place to make community engagement a major theme defining the institution—even though there is still significant work to be done). And the process of applying for that classification is not really requesting a stamp of approval; it's a tool for doing some of that significant work and moving the institution closer toward the ideal.

References

Miller, V., & Scott, D. K. (2002). Filling in the moat around the ivory tower, University of Massachusetts–Amherst. In M. E. Kenny, L. A. K. Simon, K. Kiley-Brabeck, & R. M. Lerner (Eds.), *Learning to serve: Promoting civil society through service learning* (pp. 325–342). Norwell, MA: Kluwer.

Reiff, J., & Keene, A. (2012, October). Best practices for promoting student civic engagement: Lessons from the Citizen Scholars Program at the University of Massachusetts Amherst. *Journal of Higher Education Outreach and Engagement, 16*(4), 105–127. Retrieved from http://openjournals.libs.uga.edu/index .php/jheoe/article/view/905/611

Chapter Four

OUTREACH AND PARTNERSHIPS

Cornell University's Approach to Classification

Richard Kiely, Amanda Kittelberger, and Amanda Wittman

2010: Organizing a Private Land-Grant University's Response to the Application

With Cornell University's size and land-grant status, applying for the Carnegie Classification required collaboration and coordination across multiple teams of faculty and staff. In 2010, Cornell had 14 colleges and professional schools, 55 county-based cooperative extension offices, and more than 20 research centers and museums. At the time of the application, Cornell had no standard central data collection efforts related to community engagement, with the exception of those related to cooperative extension record keeping and reporting and a K–12 outreach web portal compiled through voluntary record management at the individual program level. Although Cornell's budget contained an outreach and extension line in every college and unit, there was no standard approach to assigning community engagement resources within the budget: some were assigned to an outreach and extension category, others to faculty program budgets, and still others to department budgets—with the additional potential for any combination of the three. The medical center's budget resource expenditures were significantly more complex and were primarily identifiable through grant awards and conservative budget estimates from the central finance administrator.

At the outset of the application work, Cornell's vice provost responsible for land-grant affairs identified 2 key working groups: a 3-person core team with responsibility for content selection and application writing, and a key contacts group of approximately 30 college and unit administrators who were charged with data gathering and aggregation within their colleges/units.

Generating and Mapping Data

Cornell's vice provost responsible for land-grant affairs and the vice president for student and academic services guided college- and unit-level data collection with three simple principles for outreach and partnership data.

1. Strong engagement programs/projects are large, deep, and permanent.
2. Cornell's application should represent every college and unit of the university.
3. Data/evidence used in Cornell's responses should demonstrate the geographic range (local to global) of its work and the implicit integration of the university's institutional mission with college, unit, faculty, and student priorities and interests.

In formulating Cornell's responses to the Outreach and Partnerships portion of the application, the three-person core application team took two steps to organize data. First, the team created a cross-referencing document that mapped related questions within the Carnegie Community Engagement application and identified relevant data sources. By cross-referencing questions alongside data sources, the team could quickly identify key data providers, and, in many cases, these individuals could guide thinking about the relative merits of programs and their use in response to particular questions. These more informal channels for input about Cornell's Outreach and Partnerships responses were incredibly helpful when the team was faced with increasingly standard problems—"Which program should we choose?" and "How do we justify this to the dean, vice provost, or provost over any other program?"

Second, the team created a "possible response" matrix using the three principles to organize responses that spanned geography, engagement audience, and university "owner" by structural location and role (e.g., student, faculty, cooperative extension associate). The team reviewed aggregated data documents from each college/unit and inserted data in every application question where the information might be relevant. Using the matrix, the core team looked at the frequency of examples from particular colleges and programs to ensure broad representation of the university's engagement work. In a working session with the vice provost responsible for land-grant affairs, the core team mapped Cornell's application responses question by question. The Outreach and Partnership questions were, in a sense, a series of horse trades. The mapping strategy sought to balance Cornell's engagement evidence by type/format, source/leader, and size/impact across the application questions and subquestions.

What We Got Right

The Carnegie application process had direct support from the president and the provost. The president submitted Cornell's application and both the president and the provost corresponded within the university during the drafting process and later in the application submission. Senior administrators at the vice president and vice provost level reviewed Cornell's planned response and provided very useful input prior to response writing.

The core work team organized all application documentation on a centrally supported online data management system, called Confluence. Confluence allowed for layered security, providing a chance for every participant in the application process to see and review the majority of the university's application materials. From the beginning, the vice provost responsible for land-grant affairs and the vice president for student and academic services adopted a "more is more" approach to including faculty and staff input and advice throughout the drafting process. In addition to the main working group of approximately 30, supporting efforts on the Ithaca and New York City campuses extended to approximately 120 people.

When soliciting data and evidence from the colleges and units, the core work team asked for direct contact information for every person whose work was cited. This contact information was critical; during the writing process, the core team of three frequently went directly to the data source for assistance or clarification instead of working through the key contact.

One staff member working for the vice provost responsible for land-grant affairs was given primary responsibility for the Carnegie application project with no other major project conflicts during 10 weeks of application work. The chance to focus on the application and on the scope and relative merits of the data made a difficult thought problem much less daunting. Without a doubt, Cornell's 10-week work timeline was challenging. But by and large, between the strong support of Cornell's senior leadership and the goodwill and excitement of the people who do outreach and partnership work at Cornell, the task of completing a successful application was simply a lot of work. Because the material was there, the effort was an exercise in organization, strong writing, and keeping lots of advisers engaged at the proverbial worktable.

Finally, Cornell's process created ongoing conversations about its community engagement work and an increased interest from deans and associate deans in accountability for the university's outreach mission at the college/unit level. This was an exciting development for Cornell; faculty, staff, and administrators across the colleges and units were energized by the volume and range of activities. Faculty found it encouraging to see firsthand that they were "not alone" and to learn from colleagues' experiences and, frankly, their funding expertise. The key contacts group—associate deans and senior leaders across colleges and units—remained the central administration's "go to" people for two to three years after the classification award. The raised profile, for outreach and partnerships in particular, made collegial networking more seamless and more productive. This widespread network helped to form a foundation for positive and sustained organizational change beginning with the inception of the Center for Community-Engaged Learning and Research (expanded and later renamed the Office of Engagement Initiatives), Engaged Cornell (discussed later in this chapter), and the creation of a comprehensive public engagement structure.

Reflections on Improvement

As an institution seeking re-classification, there is much to be learned from how we managed the application process for first-time Carnegie classification. We highlight here some of the areas where the application process could be improved the next time around.

Establish similar definitions for how community engagement activity is assigned in budgets across Cornell. With more consistency in definitions, criteria and budget assignments made at the department, program, and even the college level, our efforts to catalog Cornell's total university investment would have been more straightforward in 2010. A uniform approach to definitions, criteria, and budget assignments also provides a secondary catalog for faculty and program activity if needed.

Designate a core working group member from cooperative extension. Given organization and staffing in 2010, it was not feasible for a Cornell-based cooperative extension staff member to participate as an assigned and regular member of the core working group. Instead, two administrative associate directors interacted with the core working group both individually and together. Although the system worked fine, it may have been less efficient for the extension administration's effort, and the core working group lost the benefit of a dedicated extension perspective in all discussions.

Identify "likely suspects" for responses earlier in the process to allow time to explore how programs interact or affect each other. One result of Cornell's condensed 10-week summer timeline was that the core working group was limited in its ability to explore how engagement activities, participants, and thought leaders were leveraging each other's ideas, sharing knowledge, and communicating lessons learned. With a more detailed understanding of how program and activity cross-pollination was working, Cornell's senior leadership team would have been able to use the Carnegie application process as an even stronger springboard for strategic thinking and long-term planning.

From Classification to Re-Classification: A Catalyst for Renewing a Vision for Service-Learning and Community Engagement

Preparing for and receiving the Carnegie Classification in 2010 was an important recognition of Cornell's enduring commitment to community-engaged learning and research. Importantly, rather than an end goal, the Carnegie application process was catalytic and seen by our leadership team as an opportunity to reflect on and renew our commitment to our land-grant mission. Along with being a partly private, Ivy League, and doctoral-granting research institution, Cornell's land-grant status roots public engagement in Cornell's institutional DNA from its founding in 1865. By undertaking the Carnegie Classification process, Cornell's leadership centrally identified, for the first time, inconsistencies and gaps in how

Cornell staff, faculty, administrators, and students understood the land-grant mission, community engagement activities, public scholarship, outreach, and partnership with local and global communities. It became clear Cornell did not have a common definition of *community engagement*, nor did it have sufficiently resourced systems to monitor and evaluate community engagement activities university-wide, including the quality and impact of outreach and partnerships.

The 2010 Carnegie Classification effort provided an opportunity for leadership to develop a consistent and systematic approach to monitoring, assessing, and evaluating quality community-engaged curriculum, research, and partnerships. It prompted Cornell to take a more proactive, aligned, strategic, and systematic approach to better monitor, understand, and improve community-engaged teaching, learning, and research activities at Cornell. There was broad agreement that such an undertaking required more than a symbolic commitment from administrative leadership and that additional resources and staffing would be required to ensure an infrastructure for supporting existing and new community engagement programs.

Along with the Carnegie Classification process, a number of other important university-wide activities propelled public engagement to the foreground of Cornell's vision for the future—namely, the university's Middle States Commission reaccreditation and a university-wide strategic planning effort. From 2008 to 2009, Cornell's leaders crafted the university's *Strategic Plan 2010–2015*, which designated public engagement as a critical goal. The plan delineated objectives outlining expectations for the design, implementation, and assessment of service-learning and community engagement (SLCE) activities, courses, programs, and administrative structures. In addition, the university received funding (2010–2011) from the Einhorn Family Charitable Trust for a proposal charting the future of service-learning at Cornell, ultimately leading to additional funding supporting a large-scale public engagement initiative at Cornell.

After Classification

Cornell decided early on that its program planning approach for SLCE should be relational (Palmer, Zajonc, & Scribner, 2010; Sandmann, Kiely, & Grenier, 2009). That is, leaders felt deeply that Cornell's approach should be driven by values of inclusion and collaboration, informed by actively reaching out to, engaging with, and listening to a broad and diverse range of stakeholders (e.g., administration, faculty, students, staff, community members, national experts in SLCE).

As part of planning efforts and based on gaps identified and data gathered in Cornell's Carnegie Classification application process, an early activity was to undertake a systematic inventory of outreach and partnerships with the following aims:

- Understand better who was involved in SLCE in each of the colleges
- Document courses offered and their definitions of *SLCE*
- Determine criteria and processes for approving, tracking, and assessing quality SLCE
- Note SLCE exemplars and the attributes making them exemplars
- Describe the key challenges to success
- Identify supports necessary to improve the existing SLCE efforts and meet challenges

At the time, there was no question that faculty, staff, and students were engaged in high-quality SLCE at Cornell, and the Carnegie Classification affirmed that Cornell was a highly engaged institution. Yet, to further institutionalize its outreach and partnership work, Cornell needed to capture, more fully and systematically, how and how well it was engaging in high-quality SLCE. Cornell's relational approach was meant to learn more about the type and quality of SLCE across Cornell and to develop a system to consistently define, identify, maintain, support, and share knowledge about SLCE with internal and external audiences.

With the information gathered about SLCE activities and the contacts from the Carnegie application, Cornell's efforts started with approaches to internal outreach and partnerships. Service-learning and public engagement (SLPE) leaders developed collaborative relationships with faculty, students, and staff in each of the colleges, Cooperative Extension, and other units on campus that might support or have a strong connection to SLCE (i.e., units supporting community service, service-learning, undergraduate research, diversity, international programs, and teaching excellence). From a leadership standpoint, we were wary of imposing specific definitions, criteria, and policies from our individual experiences or from what we knew from the field. Rather, SLPE leaders sought to craft definitions, criteria, and policies based on emerging evidence from engagement with diverse stakeholders across campus.

Next, SLPE leaders turned attention to meeting, convening, and developing relationships with practitioners and stakeholders in colleges and units across campus (including deans, associate deans, and educational policy committees) to gain an understanding of the language and definitions used for SLCE and then to set parameters for what constituted SLCE and for monitoring and assessing in a more systematic manner. By the end of 2014, Cornell had fairly broad acceptance for the term *public engagement* as the most inclusive language describing community-based teaching, learning, and research activities, and the institution had developed a set of definitions describing distinct types of public engagement activities—very much aligned with Boyer's (1990) *Scholarship Reconsidered*. In addition, internal outreach and relationship-building over the period of the initial three-year planning gift led to over 500 meetings with individual faculty, as well as presentations and partnerships with over 20 units on campus in support of SLCE. With SLPE leaders, administrators in 8 colleges developed numerous relationships with faculty, gained better understanding of SLCE partnerships, and supported SLCE professional development programs for students, faculty, and staff. Last, collaborative efforts with the Office of Institutional Research and Planning led to a decision to embed questions in student surveys so that Cornell would better understand participation trends in community service and service-learning activities. In parallel, work with the university registrar produced a more systematic process for tracking service-learning courses in each of the colleges and on agreement for the language of community-engaged learning (CEL) along with a set of university-wide criteria for approving and designating CEL courses.

In 2014, Cornell received a major gift alongside the university's funding campaign and Cornell launched the Engaged Cornell initiative to, over a 10-year period (2015–2025), "establish community engagement and real-world learning experiences as the hallmark of the Cornell undergraduate experience" (Walters, 2014). The major gift generated significant visibility and excitement at Cornell and in the field. With the substantial infusion of resources, Cornell has high expectations for scaling up curricula, student opportunities, and community partnerships. Increased funding has already provided opportunities for hiring additional staff who have developed communication platforms and the data management system necessary for meeting the original 5 objectives described in Cornell's strategic plan, as well as monitoring and tracking the achievement of key performance indicators described in the 10-year Engaged Cornell initiative.

Planning Ahead for the 2020 Re-Classification

As Cornell begins to organize toward the 2020 application, it is taking steps to build on the work done for the 2010 application and to consider the university's resulting public engagement infrastructure and growth in the context of the upcoming re-classification. A staff member new since 2010 will coordinate the Carnegie re-classification effort as before. Although Cornell has significantly deepened community engagement efforts over the past 10 years, there is ongoing leadership recognition that compiling, sifting, and telling the story with data and in an authentic and meaningful way is complicated and time consuming. Decision makers are hopeful that decisions being made now will help Cornell be as prepared for the re-classification process as it can be.

Cornell will use multiple strategies to address the Outreach and Partnerships section of the 2020 framework. The first key strategy is an intentional process to build and maintain relationships with units across campus who place partnerships and outreach at the center of their work. A new physical space, the Engaged Cornell Hub, houses nine programs and units supporting public engagement, and it serves as one strategy for relationship-building between units and between supported liaison positions at Engaged Cornell and Cornell Cooperative Extension. Cornell expects the strengthened relationships, along with a university-wide virtual communication platform, to help us gather and regularly communicate pertinent information on CEL opportunities and community collaborations across campus.

The second key strategy has been to establish a community partnership committee including staff, faculty, and local community partners tasked with developing a set of tools to assist with developing reciprocal partnerships and assessing both the quality and impact of the partnership. Additionally, Cornell has created committees to coordinate global partnerships and local, community-driven efforts. By stepping back and letting community members identify their needs and assets in how they would like to work with Cornell, we will be better equipped to document and describe the key qualities, attributes, principles, and dimensions of quality community-campus partnerships.

Third, we have designed a number of funding mechanisms supporting the development of community-engaged curricula, research, and partnerships, with a "big-tent" approach to how *community* is defined and understood. This diverse array of funding opportunities requires assessment and reporting of student learning and community impact along with resources to support professional development for faculty incorporation of good practices into course design, research, and partnerships. This funding strategy will enhance the quality and consistency of outreach and partnership activities, as well as our ability to document them.

Conclusion: The Importance of Planning and Preparation

As we consider the next steps for the 2020 re-classification, we recognize the importance of recruiting a strong team of faculty and staff steeped in community engagement, as well as assessment colleagues from across the university. We will draw from the perspectives of multiple community partners involved with Engaged Cornell. Leadership and support will most likely be provided by the vice provost responsible for land-grant affairs. To address our earlier conclusion about the value of identifying "likely suspects" for responses earlier in the process to allow time to explore how programs have interacted with or affected each other, we will create the team for Carnegie 2020 in the academic year before the framework is released. This timing should allow us to undertake a thorough gap analysis and spend 2017–2018 identifying data and partnership stories that represent the diversity of SLCE at Cornell.

Cornell expects to face organizational conditions that will impact its re-classification application. The first, not at all unique to Cornell, is that we have gone through tremendous leadership transitions and staff changes since 2010. None of the administrative and staff leaders involved in both the visioning and execution of the Carnegie application remain at Cornell. Like many other institutions, we remain aware of the ways our organizational changes have impacted the systems and processes for the design, implementation, and evaluation of community engagement broadly and for the Carnegie application process specifically.

Second, and possibly more unique to Cornell, is how we will negotiate metrics and reporting between activities related to Engaged Cornell and those occurring outside the parameters of Engaged Cornell leadership (e.g., state-funded Cooperative Extension). Although the Office of Engagement Initiatives is a coordinating unit for community engagement, the reality is that it is not positioned to document all of the community engagement activities at Cornell. Community engagement at Cornell will always be a complex, dynamic, and evolving story. The Carnegie Community Engagement Re-Classification will be a useful and welcome opportunity to reflect on how to best represent and share Cornell's story. Cornell is energized by the abundant opportunities supported through the Engaged Cornell initiative and it concurrently recognizes its responsibility to systematically document findings about Cornell's community engagement more broadly. The Carnegie Community Engagement framework will provide Cornell with just what its title says—a framework to demonstrate what is working, what isn't, and what else can be done to deepen community engagement, along with a platform to share the ongoing SLCE journey and lessons learned with a wider institutional audience.

References

Boyer, E. (1990). *Scholarship reconsidered*. Menlo Park, CA: Carnegie Foundation for the Advancement of Teaching.

Palmer, P., Zajonc, A., & Scribner, M. (2010). *The heart of higher education: A call to renewal*. San Francisco, CA: Jossey-Bass.

Sandmann, L., Kiely, R., & Grenier, R. (2009). Program planning in service-learning: A neglected dimension. *Michigan Journal of Community Service Learning, 15*(2), 17–33.

Walters, K. (October 6, 2014). University launches "Engaged Cornell" with $50 million gift. *Cornell Chronicle*. Retrieved from http://news.cornell.edu/stories/2014/10/university-launches-engaged-cornell-50-million-gift

Chapter Five

KEY LESSONS AND GUIDING QUESTIONS

First-Time Classification

Georgina Manok

Map Campus Stakeholders and Their Powers and Interests

Stakeholder mapping and particularly power mapping in your institution is a key step as you begin to plan for classification. Your awareness of the relationships, power structures, interests, and resources involved will help you navigate and communicate the process as well as ensure stakeholder buy-in. Consider the following questions before you begin the application process:

- Who are the constituents on campus championing community engagement?
- Who are the key players affecting those constituents and campus units?
- Who might/will be the most resistant to the classification? What is important to them? How can the classification process contribute to what they value?

- What kind of relationships has your campus established with community partners? How will they have a voice in the classification process?

Although the classification is about your institution, avoid excluding community partners in your mapping. Partner input is a valuable component of community engagement and collaboration is essential for the classification process.

Carefully Choose the Framing and Positioning of the Classification

After stakeholder and power mapping, choosing the type of framing for the classification (self-study, accreditation, award) will determine how your institution perceives and engages with the application process. You may want to consider tailoring the framing to different constituencies on your campus. As you begin planning for framing and communicating the classification process, ask yourself some initial questions:

- How is the Community Engagement Classification best framed on your campus?
- Will it be beneficial or counterproductive to use different framing with different stakeholder groups (e.g., faculty versus senior administrators versus community)?
- Which champion on campus will lead to the highest engagement in the process?

Avoid hastily planning this stage. The classification is not a two-person endeavor, and different stakeholders may respond to different framing. It is a campus-wide collaboration that may be led by a small team despite involving a large number of stakeholders. Whatever the constellation of your team, it should be broader than the community engagement office.

Collect *Community Engagement* Definition(s) on Your Campus

You may find several definitions of *community engagement* across different constituencies and units on your campus. As you reflect on community engagement in your mission and institutional strategic plans, it is useful to ask the following questions:

- Does your campus have a unified definition for *community engagement*?
- If so, what is your campus definition's proximity to the Carnegie definition?
- If not, is the classification process an opportunity to fashion one, or to identify the need to fashion one and begin the process?

Avoid excluding departments, colleges, offices, and research centers on campus that have different definitions; they may provide strategic insights, valuable data, and strong evidence in support of your application and beyond. Bringing them into the process creates the opportunity to work toward collective understanding and mutually shared goals.

Form and Train a Strong Core Group With a Long-Term Vision

The application process is designed to be an ongoing process beyond receiving the classification. Although a successful application could be your short-term objective, it is important to strategically plan the process with a long-term perspective. Selecting the right individuals who are well versed in community engagement and who are capable of forming strong partnerships and collaborative rapport with units on your campus is essential. As you plan your team and application strategy, you can ask the following questions:

- Are members of your core team educated on or aware of training opportunities such as the Carnegie Academy and other workshops or resources available to applicant institutions?
- Is your core team familiar with community engagement and prepared to do the writing?
- Is your team accurately documenting the application, partnership formation, and data collection processes?
- Is your core team incorporating a long-term vision in forming partnerships and communications with other campus units beyond the first-time classification?

Avoid forming a core team of administrators who are not specifically familiar with community engagement work. Work toward the creation of a permanent committee that will exist after classification is done to monitor progress, continue assessment, and be prepared for reapplication.

PART TWO

RE-CLASSIFICATION

Chapter Six

FOUNDATIONAL INDICATORS

Embrace the Journey

Melissa Quan

Background

It was December 2007, and I was supposed to meet with former Fairfield University president Jeffrey von Arx about Fairfield University's host agreement with Connecticut Campus Compact. Pregnant with my second child, I had to cancel due to worse-than-usual morning sickness. I called his assistant and left my cell phone number in case he needed to reach me about the meeting. Sometime late morning, the phone rang; it was a Fairfield University number. Expecting an office colleague, I picked up the phone only to hear the voice of President von Arx, "Hello dear, I am sorry to bother you at home, especially when you are not feeling well." I was a bit startled, never expecting that the president of the university would, in fact, call me at home, but he quickly erased any anxiety with his cheerful message: Fairfield University had been awarded the 2008 Carnegie Community Engagement Classification. President von Arx had called me at home to say how happy he was, to express his gratitude for my work in steering the application process, and, of course, to check in on how I was doing. This remains one of my fondest memories from my time at Fairfield University.

Backing up a year or so from that phone call, I first became aware of the Carnegie Community Engagement Classification in 2007. Fairfield University's academic vice president at the time had asked me to attend a meeting at the College of the Holy Cross, cohosted by Campus Compact and the Carnegie Foundation for the Advancement of Teaching, to gather information about the classification and to see if Fairfield was in a position to submit a competitive application. Prior to leaving for the meeting, I received a strong suggestion from the former director of institutional research that we should not consider applying for 2008 as she felt we would not have enough evidence for a competitive application. Nonetheless, I was asked to attend, listen, and gather information for a future round.

What stood out to me from that meeting was the value of the Carnegie Community Engagement Classification as a strategic planning tool for advancing community engagement. I walked away with the message that (a) we would not have to show evidence for every element on the application (except for the Foundational Indicators), and (b) even if we did not receive the classification, the value of going through the process of taking a deep dive into our community engagement work was worth the effort and would lead to constructive outcomes. I took that message back to my supervisor and the academic vice president and made an argument for applying for 2008. As a youngish midlevel professional, and not one for muddying the waters, I remember feeling pretty nervous about pushing that recommendation. I was especially nervous when the response that came back was: "Okay, let's go for it and you will lead it." And so it began.

Context: New Classification and Re-Classification

Although the primary focus of this chapter is on the re-classification process, Fairfield University's story began with the experience of achieving the first-time classification in 2008. As a community engagement professional at a Jesuit university, I have never faced the challenge of having to make a case for the importance of community engagement or its relevance to mission. The Jesuit educational mission is rooted in the values of social justice, service, solidarity, and care for the whole person. Further, the Jesuit tradition of teaching and learning is praxis oriented and involves a cyclical process of learning that connects academic content with experience, reflection, action, and evaluation (International Commission on the Apostolate of Jesuit Education, 2000). The argument for creating an institutional infrastructure for service-learning and community engagement at Fairfield University had more to do with interest and demand than anything else. When he arrived at Fairfield University in 2004, President von Arx was clear that he would support the creation of a coordinating unit for service-learning if the faculty led the effort. So a group of faculty formed and began to organize brown bag conversations, compile resources, and outline the ideal support structure. By 2006, we had an advisory committee, a director of service-learning, and an assistant director within the Center for Faith and Public Life, a newly created center for teaching and research activity that would be directly connected with the Jesuit mission and values. With a center established, a significant level of faculty engagement, leadership support, institutional investment, and a highly collaborative campus culture, the timing and climate were right for pursuing the 2008 Carnegie Community Engagement Classification.

Although Fairfield University entered the field of higher education community engagement at a later stage in the history of the movement, we were a quick study. We turned to the literature on promising practices and learned from the trials and errors of others. We applied this same strategy to the process of applying for the 2008 Carnegie Community Engagement Classification. The recommendations from the field suggested approaching the application as a planning and self-study process, developing a steering committee to collect and analyze data, identifying a single author for the application, and celebrating and leveraging the classification if awarded. We followed that well-worn path and, thankfully, were successful.

The importance that Fairfield University placed on achieving the classification in 2008, as exemplified by the personal phone call that I received from President von Arx, played a critical role in our re-classification process. Our efforts to achieve re-classification began soon after receiving the news about our initial classification. The 2008 award letter pointed out the general strengths and weaknesses of all colleges and universities that were awarded the 2006 and 2008 classifications. Areas in need of improvement, as outlined in the letter, included (a) gathering constructive feedback from community partners, (b) institution-wide assessment of community engagement, and (c) faculty support, particularly with regard to promotion and tenure (Driscoll, 2008). Recognizing the value of the Carnegie Community Engagement Classification to university leaders, I along with other community engagement practitioners on campus leveraged the excitement and used these recommendations for improvement to develop strategies for advancing community engagement at Fairfield University.

Re-Classification: Facilitating Factors and Foundational Indicators

Although we were thrilled to receive notification of our new classification in 2008, we also quickly realized that work needed to be done in order to maintain the classification in the future. We focused on making changes to our promotion and tenure guidelines. Integrating community engagement into our promotion and tenure guidelines was something that we had been talking about at Fairfield and the Carnegie Classification provided a good reason for pursuing it; further, it had come up in the context of our accreditation process, and so there was an opportunity for cross-pollination. At a workshop hosted by the then Eastern Region Campus Compact, Kerry-Ann O'Meara had recommended paying close attention to the campus climate and readiness for change. We saw a few stars aligning in favor of the changes we wanted to facilitate.

Updating Promotion and Tenure

Fairfield University's *Guidelines and Timetable for Applications for Tenure and Promotion* is the primary document that faculty use when developing their applications for tenure and promotion and is also a resource that the Committee on Rank and Tenure consults when reviewing faculty applications. These guidelines apply to the entire university—all of the schools, departments, and interdisciplinary programs. As of 2008, the guidelines were fairly broad—there was nothing in them that excluded community engagement but also nothing that signified its value in the tenure and promotion review process. In 2010, a group of faculty, administrators, and staff began to take strategic steps toward building recognition of community engagement into the promotion and tenure guidelines in more intentional ways.

In fall 2010, the dean of the College of Arts and Sciences and dean for the Office of Academic Engagement attended an institute hosted by the Eastern Region Campus Compacts (ERCC) on the Institutionalization of Community Engagement. This institute was specifically designed for institutional leaders to discuss how community engagement factored into faculty rewards and promotion and tenure policies. Beginning in spring 2011, the Fairfield University Center for Academic Excellence, the Center for Faith and Public Life, and the Office of Academic Engagement hosted a series of events and workshops on community engagement as scholarship that sparked a campus-wide conversation on the topic that continued for over two years. The deans of the College of Arts and Sciences and the Office of Academic Engagement served on a panel to discuss their takeaways from the ERCC conference while another panel featured faculty involved with community-engaged scholarship, and several events over the course of two years featured nationally known scholars on community-engaged scholarship, including Cathy Burack, Patti Clayton, Diane Doberneck, Tim Eatman, and Cathy Jordan. Each guest hosted a professional development workshop for faculty and one for administrators. These events helped to facilitate and sustain a campus-wide conversation on community-engaged scholarship that involved key stakeholders among the faculty, staff, and administration. The events highlighted the need to address the issue through policy changes as well as professional development.

In fall 2011, the director of service-learning, associate dean of the Graduate School of Education and Allied Professions, and chair of Fairfield's Academic Council participated as a team in the ERCC Faculty Institute, titled Making It Count: Strategies for Rewarding Engaged Scholarship in Promotion and Tenure. As an outcome of this institute, the team developed a strategy to work with faculty leadership toward changes in Fairfield's guidelines on promotion and tenure. In spring 2012, Fairfield's Academic Council voted in favor of a motion to form a subcommittee to consider the inclusion of language in the faculty handbook and/or *Guidelines and Timetable for Applications for Tenure and Promotion* that recognized the importance of community-engaged scholarship. It is worth noting that the faculty member who attended the ERCC institute and who put forth the motion to the Academic Council was not a community-engaged scholar. His scholarship would more likely be considered traditional, disciplinary scholarship or, in Boyer's (1990) framework, the scholarship of discovery. However, he saw the value of community engagement and wanted to ensure that his colleagues would be recognized appropriately for their work.

The appointed subcommittee included community-engaged scholars and traditional scholars, pre-tenure and tenured faculty, faculty from the humanities and professional schools, and the director of service-learning (staff member). The subcommittee surveyed the vast literature on community-engaged scholarship and best practices at comparable institutions and developed a set of recommendations that were presented to the Committee on Rank and Tenure (a faculty handbook committee) and to the Academic Council. The recommendations included changes to the research, teaching, and service sections of the guidelines. The rationale for this was that community-engaged scholarship often (though not always) extends across traditional categories recognized by rank and tenure committees. In April 2013, Fairfield University's

Academic Council accepted the subcommittee's recommendations and passed a motion to revise the *Guidelines and Timetable for Applications for Tenure and Promotion* to include explicit language on community engagement under three primary headings: teaching accomplishments, professional accomplishments, and university and/or community service.

New England Association of Schools and Colleges

During the time of these ad-hoc efforts to revise promotion and tenure, Fairfield University was also immersed in preparing its Fifth-Year Interim Report to our regional accreditor, the New England Association of Schools and Colleges (NEASC). Two key issues addressed in the NEASC report overlapped with key areas of weakness in our 2008 Carnegie Community Engagement Classification. One issue was related to aligning faculty rewards with community-engaged teaching, research, and scholarship; the second issue related to institution-wide assessment. In addressing the assessment issue through the NEASC report, the university identified three overarching student learning goals—producing students who are (a) committed to academic excellence, (b) trained as integrative thinkers, and (c) instilled with a sense of civic and social responsibility. The third learning goal attempted to capture the impact of our academic engagement with the community. An outcome of the NEASC Interim Report was the creation of a university-wide assessment committee that currently includes a representative from the Center for Faith and Public Life. Having leaders across the university focused on developing assessment plans focused on these learning goals was incredibly beneficial when it came time to complete the 2015 re-classification application, because we were able to show evidence of institution-wide assessment efforts.

Applying for Re-Classification

I am rarely one to reinvent the wheel, so when the re-classification process opened up, I went back to my notes from 2008 and followed the same approach. I asked the vice president of academic affairs to appoint cochairs of the Carnegie Community Engagement Re-Classification Task Force (one of whom would be me) and to officially "launch" the committee with a letter to the university community. This helped to establish the importance of the process and the institution's investment in it. The task force was intentionally large, with representatives from every division and departments ranging from athletics to marketing to advancement, also including the library and various offices and centers in student affairs and academic affairs. Although large committees often require a lot of work to manage, the cochair and I saw the re-classification process as an opportunity to raise awareness about our institution's commitment to community engagement and to enlist the involvement of new people. We broke the larger task force into four smaller ones focusing on different elements of the application: (a) Leadership, Mission, and Identity; (b) Institutional Commitment and Assessment; (c) Professional Development, Roles and Rewards, and Curricular Activity; and (d) Outreach and Partnerships. We launched the task force in September 2013 and officially submitted our application in April 2014.

The year that we applied for re-classification, Campus Compact offered a Peer Development Network opportunity—a learning community for representatives from campuses applying for first-time and re-classification. The group applying for re-classification was facilitated by Lina Dostilio, then director of the Center for Community Engagement Research and Teaching at Duquesne University. It turned out to be a great space for workshopping questions, sharing strategies, discussing how best to frame responses, and streamlining a question-and-answer process with contacts at the New England Research Center for Higher Education (former host of the Carnegie Community Engagement Classification). Access to these important external resources was critical to our success with the re-classification application.

Re-Classification Application: Foundational Indicators

The Foundational Indicators section of both the new and re-classification applications is the gateway to the rest of the application. If you are not able to answer yes to the Foundational Indicator questions, then you are not advised to continue with the application process. The Foundational Indicators section on the re-classification application was considerably longer than the 2008 section for first-time applicants. I was a little unnerved when I first glanced over the application. Although I had anticipated needing to show progress in the key areas of faculty supports and rewards and institution-wide assessment, I had not anticipated seeing those appear in the Foundational Indicators section. Once I gathered my bearings, I felt a weight lift when I realized we could check the "yes" box on those questions. It was a moment of relief and celebration and I felt a sense of accomplishment and pride on behalf of all those who had worked on the promotion and tenure revisions.

The re-classification application was more complex than I had anticipated. There were a number of changes from the 2008 application.

Generally speaking, we were challenged to respond in more detail and to provide more evidence of our community engagement work. There was no longer the option to apply in one or both categories: curricular engagement and/or outreach. All applicants were to submit a full application. Our task force worked throughout the fall semester and the early part of spring. The subcommittees were asked to complete their data collection by December 2013 with the idea that I would begin writing the application in January 2014. The full task force met monthly in January, February, and March 2014 to review drafts of the full application in preparation for an April submission. We submitted in April, celebrated with a nice lunch, and the waiting began. In December 2014, we learned that we had earned re-classification until 2025. Phew.

Outcomes

A few regrets that I have from the re-classification process include not having community partners involved and not having a more robust celebration. I saw the Classification for Community Engagement as something that primarily benefited the university and thus did not feel as though I could ask community partners to commit their valuable time to the application process. And, if I am being perfectly honest, the task of facilitating a large task force of internal colleagues was daunting enough; the thought of adding external partners seemed too much. We have had community partners on our Service Learning Advisory Committee since 2007 and regularly gather feedback from the community through surveys and informal communications, particularly around service-learning coursework. We have learned over the years, though, that community partners often desire more opportunities to provide input into our work—for example, by making contributions to service-learning course design. In retrospect, I wish that I had been more creative in identifying ways to include community partners in the re-classification application. As for the celebration, we did have a celebratory lunch but failed to make it a university-wide celebration. We do, however, regularly reference the Community Engagement Classification with pride and use the data to inform our work, including a recent self-study of mission.

A refrain that you hear repeated in circles of folks promoting the Carnegie Community Engagement Classification is that "the reward is in the process itself." In my experience, I have found that to be true. The process of applying for the classification raised awareness on campus about community engagement, drew more people into the work, and earned the

Center for Faith and Public Life a spot on the Institutional Assessment Committee. Fairfield University launched a strategic planning process in 2014, and community engagement is an important element in various sections of the final plan, *Fairfield 2020: The Way Forward*. I think that our success with the classification likely left an impression upon campus leaders, demonstrating for them the value of community engagement and what we were capable of; further, having the classification has caught the attention of leaders recently attracted to the university, including our incoming president and new dean of the College of Arts and Sciences. For me personally, the opportunity to lead my campus through the new and re-classification processes helped me to know my institution better, see opportunities and gaps, and expand my professional network both internal and external to Fairfield University. So, for those considering new or re-classification in the future, let me add my voice to the chorus: embrace the journey.

References

Boyer, E. L. (1990). *Scholarship reconsidered: Priorities of the professoriate*. Lawrenceville, NJ: Princeton University Press.

Driscoll, A. (2008). Carnegie's Community-Engagement Classification: Intentions and insights. *Change: The Magazine of Higher Learning, 40*(1), 38–41.

International Commission on the Apostolate of Jesuit Education. (2000). Ignatian pedagogy: A practical approach. In V. Duminuco (Ed.), *The Jesuit ratio studiorum: 400th anniversary perspectives*. New York, NY: Fordham University Press.

Chapter Seven

CURRICULAR ENGAGEMENT

In the Eye of the Whirlwind

Marshall Welch

Introduction

Reflecting upon our efforts to advance community engagement at Saint Mary's College of California and to apply for the Carnegie Re-Classification initially evoked the metaphor of the "perfect storm," recalling how the combination of particular climatic conditions on our campus led to receiving the classification. Although the endeavor was often stormy, upon further reflection I questioned the accuracy and the image of a storm as that word connotes a sense of destruction and debris left in its wake. We were fortunate in that the initial application and re-application process did not result in any institutional or programmatic "damage." Instead, it is more accurate to depict the process as being in the eye of a whirlwind of activity in which we flourished. From this relatively calm center and vantage point, I can now see in retrospect the convergence and accumulative effect of at least four factors and conditions (discussed in the following four sections) whirling around our campus that brought the curricular aspect of community engagement into fruition and contributed to incremental steps that led to *earning* the Carnegie Classification in the first place.

The verb *earning* is key, as many institutions believe this is merely a matter of applying for and receiving the classification. Instead, it is much more accurate and important to clearly understand going into this process that an institution must document evidence of purpose, platforms, and programs that advance community engagement to *earn* the classification and/or re-classification (Welch, 2016). The conditions and context dictated what we did and with whom, as well as how we felt along the way. Although the focus here is on our curricular efforts, the activities described reflect the interplay of various benchmarks within the Carnegie Classification—such as infrastructure and policy. This narrative is a conversational stream of consciousness retrospection on our efforts to formalize credit-bearing engaged coursework on our campus.

Mission

I arrived at Saint Mary's College of California in 2007 as the new director of its center for community service and service-learning after serving as the director of the Lowell Bennion Community Service Center at the University of Utah. I was attracted to this Catholic liberal arts college because of its mission of social justice—a concept and two words that were not part of the lexicon or culture at a large public research university in a politically conservative state. At Saint Mary's College, the words *social justice* were actually embedded in my new job description, as it was my role to integrate social justice through service-learning into the undergraduate experience of our students. I now see institutional mission as the first significant factor and condition that was conducive to advancing community engagement.

In the context of a Catholic institution of higher education, community engagement was a vehicle for promoting social justice. As a result, it was not a hard sell to faculty or students to connect, in Ernest Boyer's (1997) words, "the rich resources of the university to our most pressing social, civic, and ethical problems" (p. 92). In fact, the college was heavily involved and invested in a variety of projects and activities (many stemming from the Office of Mission and Ministry), all deemed to be forms of community engagement to promote social justice.

However, this was all somewhat "loosey goosey," with little or no formal policy, definitions, or designation process in place. Much of it reflected a charity model and what Keith Morton (1995) would characterize as "thin service" (p. 21). Instructors were, indeed, calling *any* form of student activity off campus in the community "service-learning." Students were instructed to go by the campus center that I was now directing and "pick out a place to put in some hours." That process and expectation was soon dismantled and replaced with a greater pedagogical intentionality and emphasis on best practice through comprehensive faculty development efforts.

External Influence

The campus had undergone an external review for accreditation the year prior to my arrival. The review team took note of the admirable yet disjointed efforts to promote social justice as well as the fact that the institution as a whole did not have a mechanism for coordinating or monitoring these cocurricular and curricular programs. As a result, there was a formal recommendation in the final report to establish a centralized coordinating committee or body to effectively and efficiently manage efforts. This, in turn, created the second significant condition and factor that eventually led to the campus's formalization of community engagement that resulted in earning the Carnegie Classification.

There was now an external impetus and motivation to comply with a formal accreditation review recommendation that validated these efforts. It's difficult to discern whether this was a "carrot" or a "stick" motivating action. Nevertheless, from this recommendation, the campus instituted a Social Justice Coordinating Committee comprising faculty representatives from each of the four schools on campus, staff from various offices within mission and ministry, student life, and other units on campus. In my role as director, I was charged to chair this committee and its efforts. Later, my office and staff did most of the logistical work that eventually led to terminating the committee when the college determined it had successfully met and completed its charge.

Campus and Faculty Consensus

The first task of the committee was to define and characterize how the institution's mission of social justice could be advanced through the educational experience. Poster paper was tacked on the wall of a large conference room as the committee worked to create an institutional definition and characterization of *social justice*. The group identified three main mechanisms: (a) social justice, (b) service-learning, and (c) community-based research (CBR). It was collectively decided that we needed an institutional definition for each, as well as benchmarks that could be used to formally designate and categorize programs and activities. The committee worked collectively to create operational definitions. Curiously, *social justice* was characterized as more or less a "traditional" course or club/organization that *studied* social issues but did not necessarily incorporate praxis or include any activities for students to complete outside the classroom in the community. The campus definition of *service-learning* reflected many of the key components found in the professional literature, including mutuality, implementing reflection before/during/after service, tying service activities directly to learning objectives coupled with goals of the community partner, and a theoretical and/or theological foundation. Similarly, the campus definition of *community-based research* included the essential tenets articulated by Strand, Marullo, Cutforth, Stoecker, and Donohue (2003), though it is interesting to note that CBR at Saint Mary's College was typically implemented by students within a service-learning class rather than a scholarly activity conducted by an individual faculty member.

The next step of generating benchmarks for each of the definitions was turned over to faculty, which, in turn, became the third important condition in this collective climate of community engagement. My staff and I identified any and all instructors teaching a course that resembled anything remotely similar to service-learning. A total of 17 faculty members attended an afternoon retreat that included lunch—embracing the mantra "If they eat—they meet." In this setting, poster paper was again arranged around the walls and participants were invited to describe or define *service-learning, social justice, community-based research*, as well as what each of these "were not." After a flurry of the cognitive and physical aerobics of moving about the room, we collectively "unpacked" the information from each of the poster papers. I had prepared and projected PowerPoint slides containing definitions and best practice for each of the terms from the professional literature and then cross-referenced them with the collective brainstorming that had just occurred on the poster paper. Amazingly, we were able to wordsmith definitions that were later adopted as formal, official definitions for our campus.

Another early task of mine as the new director was to establish a faculty advisory group. My staff and I reviewed the list of instructors from each of the four schools on campus and identified respected faculty leaders doing this work. We invited them to serve in this capacity, describing their role and responsibility as first developing benchmarks that they would later use to review and designate courses. We were fortunate in establishing the proverbial "dream team" of what could be considered engaged faculty who were committed not only to this work but also to doing it well.

They did, indeed, develop a cluster of benchmarks for service-learning, social justice, and CBR. This process proved fortuitous as it was used as a model for a campus-wide initiative to establish a core curriculum consisting of 12 learning outcomes that all undergraduate students were expected to successfully complete before graduation. Community engagement was included as one of the 12 learning objectives, suggesting that the ethos and priority had truly been institutionalized on campus.

During a "town hall meeting" to discuss the core curriculum, a highly respected faculty member stood and quite literally held up a page containing the designation benchmarks for service-learning our advisory committee had developed as a model and example of how each of the 12 learning objectives would be characterized. Eventually, another task force was convened to officially define and characterize *community engagement* as part of the core curriculum. The definition included benchmarks that were used by a faculty committee to designate courses and cocurricular activities that met the criteria. Courses already designated as service-learning or CBR automatically fell under the umbrella of community engagement. This is significant as it illustrates a faculty-driven conceptualization and institutionalization of community engagement for the institution. Another significant development was the recommendation of faculty to compensate students completing community engagement for travel to and from community partner sites and for the cost of background checks and health screenings. As such, the institution made a substantial financial commitment to defray these expenses with my office and staff charged to oversee the complicated logistics that ensued. The college was literally "putting its money where its mouth was"—another significant benchmark within the Carnegie Classification.

My staff and I then gathered existing syllabi we had on file and invited faculty to submit syllabi for review using the new institutional benchmarks. We carefully and diplomatically explained the role of the advisory committee (emphasizing the word *advisory*) would not only be to officially designate courses but to also provide a friendly critique and advice on aspects of the course descriptions that did not fully or clearly address each of the benchmarks. My office was to provide technical support to faculty whose course descriptions and/or syllabi didn't clearly or fully reflect the benchmarks. Upon revision and review by the committee, the course was designated and listed by the registrar. To streamline the process, the faculty advisory committee recommended that my office develop and implement regularly scheduled faculty development cohorts to help faculty conceptualize, implement, and assess community engagement activities such as service-learning and CBR.

Again, faculty development is a significant component to document in the application process for the Carnegie Classification. The institution provided funds as a stipend for faculty who not only participated in the comprehensive faculty development but also successfully developed and submitted course syllabi that met official designation benchmarks.

Centralized Coordination

This led to the fourth and final factor—centralized coordination—that significantly influenced the formalization of community engagement on our campus, which in turn helped us with our re-classification application. Although my office existed prior to my arrival, its main focus was on cocurricular student programs such as Bonner Leaders, Jumpstart, and Saturday Service Days. Any involvement my staff had with faculty doing what they assumed to be service-learning was peripheral, generally helping instructors find a community partner.

Over time, as the new community engagement component within the core curriculum was implemented, our office was expected to coordinate an array of support including providing faculty development and technical support, archiving course syllabi, brokering partnerships with community agencies, facilitating risk assessment, reimbursing student travel, arranging background checks and health screenings (e.g., tuberculosis tests), and obtaining memos of understanding, along with a host of other activities including work with community partners. Likewise, our office served as a clearinghouse where important information such as lists of courses, faculty, and community partners were now archived through the Social Justice Coordinating Committee and readily accessible. This expanded role and responsibility of our office in and of itself reflected many of the criteria and benchmarks for receiving the Carnegie Classification.

This background information illustrates that the process does not occur overnight. The whirlwind of campus climatic conditions created a sense of institutional inertia that we capitalized on. Likewise, this narrative articulates the behaviors and actions that were taken to advance this work on campus and applying/reapplying for the Carnegie Classification. Efforts were mission driven—a critical component within the Carnegie benchmarks. Similarly, the campus community and faculty were involved in the early discussions to define and characterize this work to give it academic credibility. My office did the "heavy lifting" and, therefore, faculty and community partners felt supported and heard. This garnered respect for and confidence in my office and staff that, in turn, provided our office a degree of agency and autonomy when it came to advancing this work and completing the application for the Carnegie Classification. Given the campus had just completed an arduous accreditation review and established the new core curriculum, there was an element of "initiative fatigue" in which the campus administration and faculty gladly trusted and turned the application process over to my office.

The Application and Reapplication Process

Coincidentally, the annual application for the President's Honor Roll for Community Engagement was looming large around the same time we began the reapplication for the Carnegie Classification. I sought and gained permission from my vice provost to apply for both recognitions. He saw the value of both and encouraged my office to proceed. My associate director and I decided to take a "divide and conquer" approach in which I took the lead on the Carnegie reapplication and she took the lead on the Honor Roll application. Independently, each of us compiled the necessary information and data required for both applications that were now readily available in our office database, plugging in data to our respective applications. During our regular weekly check-in, we would debrief and discuss our individual progress as well as problem-solve and share data. Likewise, each of us consulted with individual staff members in our office or collectively during our weekly staff meeting to compile accurate numbers and information. As such, we did not have a campus team of representatives from departments and units working on the applications—this simplified the process.

There were, however, instances when I had to consult with specific programs to get updated information or clarification before including it in the application. This, as will be described, presented some challenges. In the meantime, there was essentially no need or reason for in-depth consultation with any other individuals or offices on campus, as our office was the hub of community engagement efforts on campus. We had our finger on the pulse of community engagement for the college. This, in and of itself, is the beauty and utility of having at least one centralized coordinating office for community engagement. Given the size of our campus, there is no need for other similar offices. However, I can see why and how a larger institution might have several offices doing similar work, hence requiring a collective effort to compile the information. As such, neither of us experienced any real frustration or political angst—only the pressure of meeting deadlines—that is, until the topic of student teaching and internships surfaced.

Semantics

I was in teacher education prior to transitioning into the field of service-learning and community engagement. Therefore, I can attest to the tension that commonly exists between professional preparation programs that require practica experiences for preprofessionals, such as student teaching for teacher candidates, and the engaged pedagogy of service-learning. I confess my own earlier cavalier confusion and somewhat dismissive attitude toward service-learning nearly 20 years ago. After all, my teacher candidates were "out in the community" learning. Over time, I came to understand and appreciate the nuanced difference in the purpose and ethos of community engagement and experiential education as practiced in professional preparation programs. The main, and perhaps most, significant difference is the student-centric focus of practica in which preprofessionals demonstrate mastery of specific skills and knowledge to obtain certification and licensure in contrast to the mutual goals and benefits of a partnership in which community agencies are coeducators that cocreate new knowledge with students and faculty. Thus, we were faced with a conundrum as to whether or not to include student teaching and internships in the application for the Carnegie Classification. We reached a compromise.

The teacher education program at Saint Mary's College was a postbaccalaureate program that embedded the institution's mission of social justice into its practica experience for teacher candidates. The School of Education established a policy that all student teaching experiences would occur in underresourced Title I schools to promote an awareness of social issues and conditions to reflect the institution's commitment to social justice. Many of the courses and seminars included the Freirian theory of praxis (Freire, 1970) in an attempt to socialize preprofessional teachers that they were agents of change. College faculty worked closely with principals and district administrators to establish long-standing, culturally competent partnerships and experiences that would be mutually beneficial to the school and not merely a convenient "placement" where college students could complete their requirements. Consequently, we decided to include teacher education in the profile and application process.

However, using the Carnegie Foundation's own definition of *community engagement*, we made the executive decision not to include internships in our application for at least two reasons. First, the National Association of Colleges and Employers (NACE) defined *internships* as

> a form of experiential learning that integrates knowledge and theory learned in the classroom with practical application and skills development

in a professional setting. Internships give students the opportunity to gain valuable applied experience and make connections in professional fields they are considering for career paths; and give employers the opportunity to guide and evaluate talent. (National Association of Colleges and Employers, 2015)

Thus, we concluded that, although being valuable learning experiences, internships lacked the spirit and ethos of mutual benefit of community engagement articulated in the Carnegie definition. Internships were student-centric with little to no benefit to organizations or corporations. Second, unlike the intentional deliberation that occurred when formally conceptualizing service-learning, social justice, and CBR, individual departments and programs were independently implementing their own interpretations of what an internship should include or entail. As such, there was no campus-wide definition or set of benchmarks to ensure a consistent framework.

Therefore, the format and quality of internships ranged from a robust program comprising careful selection and approval of internship sites, faculty supervision, weekly readings and discussions during faculty-led seminars, on-site supervisors, and learning objectives to allowing students to find their own internship site and merely "shadow" workers there with little or no supervision or instructional support. This generated both a degree of resentment and awareness. In one aspect, we offended some colleagues and departments by insinuating their efforts were not robust. In another, this created an institutional need to explore and formalize internships. Unlike the consensus-driven approach to institutionalize service-learning and community engagement, the college had no central office to coordinate or oversee internships.

Outcomes

The administration was pleased when we received the Carnegie Classification. It was announced in both on- and off-campus publications and notifications. The outside, objective validation provided not merely cachet but also credibility to our efforts. Administrators and faculty took notice and surmised that there "must be something to all this community engagement business after all" and that it was not just the agenda of a particular office on campus. The recognition also provided leverage for additional resources and support. At the same time, notification of the award included areas that needed continued work and attention. For our campus, that meant addressing and including this work in the promotion and tenure process coupled with faculty recruitment and hiring and the ever-ongoing challenge of assessing the impact of community engagement.

So, in hindsight, it became clear to me that applying for and receiving the Carnegie Classification for Community Engagement are not merely a matter of "hunkering down" to complete an online application form. Campuses will be fooling themselves and only be disappointed if they presume that *receiving* the classification comes after submitting an application. It is a long, ongoing evolutionary process and practice. For institutions just now beginning to explore and advance community engagement, the Carnegie Classification application process may, in fact, be a readiness assessment tool and opportunity that can guide a campus in its efforts. Instead of actually submitting the application, a team can use it to chart a direction and plan over the course of a few years. In many ways, this is what we did at Saint Mary's College, without the benefit of having the actual application document to guide us. We essentially had an institutionalization compass (Welch, 2016) consisting of a "top-down" institutional mission coupled with a "bottom-up" critical mass of faculty helping to move this agenda forward. The cultural values of social justice within a Catholic college combined with the infrastructure of a centralized coordinating office were equally influential. The classification in and of itself is merely an acknowledgment of concerted efforts that already exist to integrate purpose, platforms, and programs that advance the cocreation of knowledge and practice that benefits students, faculty, the institution, and the community.

References

Boyer, E. L. (1997). *Selected speeches: 1979–1995*. Princeton, NJ: Carnegie Foundation for the Advancement of Teaching.

Freire, P. (1970). *Pedagogy of the oppressed*. New York, NY: Continuum.

Morton, K. (1995). The irony of service: Charity, project, and social change in service-learning. *Michigan Journal of Community Service Learning, 2*(1), 19–32.

National Association of Colleges and Employers. (2015). *Position statement: U.S. internships*. Retrieved from http://www.naceweb.org/advocacy/position-statements/united-states-internships.aspx

Strand, K., Marullo, S., Cutforth, N., Stoecker, R., & Donohue, P. (2003). *Community-based research and higher education: Principles and practice*. San Francisco, CA: Jossey-Bass.

Welch, M. (2016). *Engaging higher education: Purpose, platforms, and programs*. Sterling, VA: Stylus.

Chapter Eight

OUTREACH AND PARTNERSHIPS

Making the Juice Worth the Squeeze

Emily M. Janke

Introduction

Reflecting on my experience as the chair and lead writer of our campus's efforts to reclassify for the Elective Community Engagement Classification, I revisited some notes I'd made to myself about the process. The first note was dated 14 months before the application deadline. It read: "Who will be writing this? LOTS of time. Can I get a grad student to help?" I read that note now with a sense of astonishment at the opening question. Clearly, I was anxious and possibly hoping that the work of reclassifying wouldn't fall to my small office of me and one staff member. My note also suggests that I knew that this was my responsibility and that I felt I needed to get "A LOT" of help.

Thinking about it now, that seems like an absurd response. I had taken the positions of special assistant for community engagement and then as the director of the Institute for Community and Economic Engagement (reporting to the chief research officer) a few years previously, in part, but precisely, *to* collect data about community engagement across the University of North Carolina at Greensboro's (UNCG's) campus. Describing how we collected data for the Outreach and Partnerships section necessarily includes description of how we systematically collected data across the university for the Carnegie process.

The effort to collect data across the campus was named in the university's strategic plan implementation report in order to support community engagement. I had coauthored the report, and data collection had become a key focus of the institute that I directed. Not only did I *know* that applying for recertification would fall to my office, I *wanted* to lead this effort and had *planned* for it since I had first joined the vice chancellor's office three years prior.

Institutional Context

So my response was an emotional one; my head knew the strategic importance of the re-classification *process* to build understanding, buy-in, and connections across campus for community engagement, as well as the resulting (if successful) public recognition as a community-engaged institution. Yet I was anxious. My feeling of anxiety was likely stemming from my worry about faculty and staff members' responses to yet one more "ask" for data. The last few years had been especially heavy with regard to strategic planning, institutional accreditation, and various reports and requests for information about different aspects of the university. Many of these included community engagement and public service activities.

At the time in which the note to myself was written, we were three years into our campus strategic plan, in which faculty and staff were extensively involved. The implementation committee for the goal "support community-engaged scholarship" had spent considerable time drafting its plan and budget. Additionally, faculty and staff had just finished their contributions as part of the institutional reaccreditation through the Southern Association of Colleges and Schools, which also required evidence of institutional effectiveness around "community/public service." Furthermore, as a University of North Carolina (UNC) system member campus, we were required to submit data on campus-wide community engagement and public service as part of an initiative to "make the residents of North Carolina fall back in love with its institutions of higher education" (Janke, 2014). Each of these efforts was consuming. And these were in addition to the numbers and stories required annually for the President's National Honor Roll for Community Service.

Although there was some overlap among items requested, each report requested a different piece of data as each was for a different purpose (e.g., planning, accreditation, recognition). As I skimmed over the items in the reapplication process and reviewed what UNCG had submitted for the first-time classification, it was clear to me that there was much more to collect across all areas of the documentation framework, and a different kind of writing was required for successful re-classification. This is because the re-classification application requires that institutions describe *what has changed* since the last application, providing evidence of these changes through a full audit of each dimension within the framework.

Devising a Plan

Critically, I did receive the help of a graduate assistant. This was an important resource. Working with the graduate assistant and a staff member, we created a table with four columns: the indicator named in the framework, who has or knows where to find relevant data, existing sources of data that we already know about or have already collected for other activities, and the name of the person or office that will take responsibility for collecting the data needed to write a complete response. In almost all cases, my office was the lead in data collection, although a number of reporting areas required faculty and staff from other units and offices to provide information, particularly in the curricular engagement section, such as undergraduate research and international programs.

As we developed this plan, I kept in mind a key question that guided the work of the UNC Metrics Taskforce (which I chaired): Is the juice worth the squeeze (Janke, 2014)? In other words, is the information that we collect valuable in some meaningful and strategic way that makes it worth the effort? Does the benefit outweigh the cost?

In this metaphor, the squeeze is the process—the time, the effort, and also the political cost of asking for information from faculty and staff who already have increasing administrative and reporting burdens. To make data collection as easy as possible for others, my office took the responsibility of writing the document, incorporating the components drafted by appointed writers.

Working Group

To ensure that we had the full information, as well as opportunity to stimulate conversation and provide education about what community engagement is, and also to get buy-in from offices across the institution, we created a list of people we needed to include in a working group. An invitation to the group was cosigned by the provost and me as director and included representatives from each academic unit and the graduate school, as well as key areas identified in the framework such as offices of leadership and service-learning, undergraduate research, planning and assessment, institutional research, international programs, learning communities, and first-year experience; the chairs of the undergraduate studies council and general education committees; and others who could contribute ideas about programs and data. At the start of the year, we convened approximately 20 representatives in a single meeting. At the meeting, we provided an introduction to the Carnegie application: what it is, expectations, roles, and timelines. We discussed the definition of *community engagement*, walked through various components of the documentation framework, and described the data that our office had already identified through existing reports and our own data collection efforts on community-engaged activities and partnerships. We also discussed the near-term goal of re-classification and how it aligned with and informed long-term goals of helping to identify, connect, promote, and sustain community engagement at UNCG.

Activity

Through the data collection process, we wanted to lessen the "squeeze" (the amount of effort individuals would experience in collecting and reporting data) by crowd-sourcing information among an informed group of campus representatives. In advance of the meeting, I had asked several individuals to take the lead role in collecting data and writing no more than 500 words for certain areas. At the meeting, we had two rounds of crowd-sourcing discussions structured similarly to a World Café format: one person (often the lead writer of a section) would facilitate 10-minute brainstorming sessions to capture sources of data or people to talk to about data related to the assigned topic. The first round focused on four areas of curricular areas of engagement: undergraduate research, internships and co-ops, scholarship of teaching and learning (SOTL), and faculty development. Topics for the tables were chosen because they were either particularly difficult for our campus to track *as related to community engagement*, or we suspected that there were more people doing community engagement than reporting it (e.g., service-learning). Committee members circulated among each of the four tables until each lead writer had collected the wisdom of the group. By the end of the two rounds walk, we had surfaced important information about what was happening where, as well as how, if at all, data was being collected.

Systematic Data Collection

The meeting also helped us to be more intentional in our systematic collection of data. Coming together as a large committee helped to create a common language and understanding about community engagement before colleagues were sent off to talk with additional individuals across campus in their own data collection efforts. We also identified places where it might be possible to insert a few questions into surveys that we already collect, or hope to collect. For example, the director of undergraduate research included questions about community-engaged research into his campus-wide survey of undergraduate research. We discussed ways in which plans for an institutional cocurricular transcript could help track cocurricular engagement.

We also shared and discussed the database that UNCG had developed the year earlier and began using in place of an online form to collect data about community engagement activities and partnerships (see Janke & Medlin, 2015, for more description of the data collection strategy). This database collected information across campus about the basic details of faculty and staff members' partnerships—who was involved, a description of the engaged activity, where the activity occurs, the topic areas or foci of study, the roles of the partners, the ways in which students were involved, and outcomes expected and/or achieved. The database was developed to help UNCG identify the landscape of its activities in and with the community and to provide a foundation for more sophisticated research, assessment, and benchmarking strategies. Having a database of regularly collected data about community engagement activities meant that we had a systematic way of collecting information from faculty and staff throughout the year as well as inputting information that we discovered as a result of data collection across all areas of the Carnegie documentation framework.

Is It Outreach or Community Engagement?

As Marshall Welch wrote in chapter 7, language can be a tricky thing. The classification framework requires that campuses report on both outreach and community engagement. Outreach describes the services and offerings provided to or for communities and the public, whereas community engagement requires reciprocal partnerships that provide mutual benefit. Both forms, outreach and community engagement, are ways that institutions of higher education contribute to the health, safety, and vibrancy of communities. Therefore, in collecting information about outreach and community engagement partnerships, we had to create systems that collected both forms of contribution but also differentiated the two forms. Our campus had begun to systematically track information about activities that are done in partnership with communities, as well as those in which activities are provided to the community by the university, several years prior to the re-classification process.

At the time of re-classification, our campus was using a database developed by the institute director and a staff member to collect community engagement activities. We used a Qualtrics survey to collect information about public service (UNCG uses the term *public service* instead of *outreach*). (Note: These two forms have since been merged into the software that was subsequently licensed as the Collaboratory.) Established definitions were helpful, if not necessary, to our data collection efforts. Our university had established them several years prior as part of efforts to support community-engaged scholarship in promotion and tenure policies (see Janke, Medlin, & Holland, 2016). We created a website to explain our data collection efforts and posted frequently asked questions (FAQs).

For the most part, faculty, staff, and administrative leadership have supported tracking community engagement partnership efforts at UNCG because collecting the data is seen and used as a means to an end. Although our campus leader's desire to reclassify as a community-engaged institution helped to create a clear and pressing rationale for why data was needed and how it would be used, tracking was never really about reporting. It was about understanding our institutional engagement portrait and telling our institution's engagement story.

Completing the Application

Using the data collected in the database, we selected examples of outreach and community engagement partnerships for the "partnership grid" that is part of the application. The stories about many of the examples had been written in other reports, news stories, or public relations efforts. I, along with the staff member and graduate student, collected these stories, refined them for the application, and shared the narrative with the partners involved to ensure accuracy. We chose examples that illustrated UNCG's efforts since 2008 to foster regional, cross-sector, and interdisciplinary scholarship. During this time UNCG had focused resources toward initiatives that contributed to the social and cultural, as well as the economic, vibrancy of the region.

The re-classification application requires institutions to compare the completed partnership grid across application years. We worked with the Office of Leadership and Service-Learning to describe the actions taken to deepen, improve, and assess partnerships. Our narrative included descriptions of programs and support offered by the office, as well as new initiatives developed by the institute for community and economic engagement. These included the Referral Desk, a portal and point source for community inquiries (broadly defined) about services and resources provided by UNCG, as well as opportunities for mutually beneficial knowledge exchange partnerships.

The ongoing curation of community engagement partnerships in the database has allowed my office to respond to requests by convening experienced community-engaged faculty and staff with community members to explore developing a shared agenda on a community-identified priority. To that end, we chose partnerships from the database that represented the work of faculty, staff, students, and community partners across the seven schools and college that make up the university and that focused on institutional and community areas of strength and priority: school learning success; culture, arts, and design; healthy people and healthy communities; and entrepreneurial partnerships. Our message throughout our outreach and partnerships narrative was that UNCG had begun to establish strategies and structures to encourage and support a stance in which it is one of many partners in the community with a desire to address relevant community priorities along with community leaders and residents.

Anxiety Relieved

It has become easier to track community engagement and public service activities. The first year was the hardest, as we had to create a community organizing strategy of interacting with groups and individuals in meetings that we set up, responding to frequently asked questions, and creating and implementing an online mechanism (online form and then database) to collect the information across campus.

In fact, each year since our initial effort, we have had faculty members and administrative staff reach out to us to share stories or ask when the information about partnerships is due. Some have even *thanked* us for requesting this information. I believe this is because, in other instances of data collection, information has gone into a "black hole"—no one sees it other than the reviewer. We actively share the information we receive through updating the university website, posting on social media, and showcasing data in various university and alumni relations materials and media. Many times these become stories shared by the chancellor to describe what community engagement looks like at a high research activity, minority-serving institution.

The next time we re-classify, I hope I will feel eager, not anxious, because I have learned that this work is important and meaningful. Although I know that there will always be some faculty and staff resistance, or at least annoyance at receiving another request for information, there are also those who will know that, in reporting on their outreach and partnership activities regularly and through established and familiar mechanisms to collect data, their stories are being told, their stories are being recognized, and their stories matter.

References

Janke, E. M. (2014). "Rekindle and recapture the love": Establishing system-wide indicators of progress in community engagement and economic development. *Michigan Journal of Community Service-Learning, 21*(1), pp. 31–42.

Janke, E. M., & Medlin, K. B. (2015). A centralized strategy to collect comprehensive institution-wide data from faculty and staff about community engagement and public service. *Metropolitan Journal, 26*(2), 125–146.

Janke, E. M., Medlin, K. B., & Holland, B. A. (2016). Intense, pervasive and shared faculty dialogue: Generating understanding and identifying "hotspots" in five days. *Metropolitan Journal 27*(2), 19–35. doi:10.18060/21124

Chapter Nine

KEY LESSONS AND GUIDING QUESTIONS

Re-Classification

Georgina Manok

Capitalize on Success

The success of your classification application will mark the first milestone in a longer journey of your institution's commitment to being a nationally recognized community-engaged campus. You should capitalize on the momentum of receiving the classification to push for further communication of the importance of the classification, institutionalizing and embedding community engagement across your campus. Guiding questions upon receiving your classification include the following:

- What will the next decade of community engagement look like for my campus in the next year, 5 years, and 10 years?
- How can we leverage the classification to push for institutional change in areas where community engagement is still underdeveloped?
- How can we add or maintain community engagement as a major component of our strategic planning to secure our commitment beyond this classification cycle?
- What data-collecting tools should we be using in the interim years to measure progress toward our community engagement goals?

Avoid treating the successful application as an endpoint. It is only the first milestone of your national community engagement recognition journey. Consider tools like the National Assessment of Service and Community Engagement and the National Institutional Inventory for Community Engagement to continue collecting data and setting and monitoring progress toward institutional change.

Revise Your Timelines and Create a Long-Term Plan

Your timeline for re-classification is 10 years. Although this may seem like a long time, institutional change can take several years and it is never too early to plan. Make sure you are not leaving this to the last year. Progress on your commitments in the first-time application and the type of evidence requested for re-classification will likely be a year-by-year implementation process. Start early, revise and evaluate your first-time classification process, collect lessons learned, and strategize what the next steps ought to be. Some guiding questions include the following:

- What commitments did we make that we need to focus on implementing in the short term?
- What areas of improvement did the first classification process highlight?
- What collaborations do we need to solidify as we plan our next decade in engagement?

Focus on commitments you have made and the weaknesses you identified in your first-time application process. You will need to provide evidence of progress in your re-classification. Share your findings in public forums and in campus media to educate the broader community about what needs to be accomplished and what is to be celebrated.

Expand the Core Group and Bring In Outside Voices

Your core group led the writing and data consolidation and selection process. It is now time to expand this group to include other key players that emerged and contributed to the application process. Make sure to maintain this group/committee as a regular standing committee. It is important to continue to expand this group's capacities and training to continue to engage in community-engaged campus-wide efforts. Keep an eye open for Carnegie academies, workshops, and conferences in your state/region.

Make sure to continue to involve your community partners in the process, and bring in outside voices to your campus who can support you in raising leadership, faculty, and staff literacy in the field. Some guiding questions include the following:

- How are we expanding our knowledge of our own institution and of the field?
- Are we investing in new skills training and expansion of our core team to create sustainability in our process?
- Is our campus leadership invested in expanding community engagement knowledge across campus?

Avoid a purely top-down approach to the process, and make sure you're increasing faculty and staff interest and knowledge in the classification to complement leadership endorsement.

Reevaluate Your Campus, Including Your *Community Engagement* Definition

As you get closer to your re-classification, reevaluate your campus and continue to actively map stakeholders and manage your relationships with them. Review areas of improvement identified in your initial classification and make sure you are keeping up with emerging trends in the field and classification updates. You can also track key players in the field such as Campus Compact or the Swearer Center at Brown University. These partners will provide you with recent trends in the field and potential changes to the framework as you get closer to the re-classification cycle. Some guiding questions include the following:

- How has our *community engagement* definition evolved in the last few years?
- Are there new trends in the field that we need to adopt? How are we keeping in touch with these developments?
- How are we working toward improving key areas that were highlighted in the initial application?

Avoid assuming that your campus and stakeholder and power maps have remained unchanged even if your leadership remained the same.

PART THREE

GATHERING AND USING
EVIDENCE

Chapter Ten

ALIGNING COMMUNITY ENGAGEMENT WITH REACCREDITATION AND STRATEGIC PLANNING

Creating a Jazz Ensemble to Orchestrate Change

Julie A. Hatcher and Stephen P. Hundley

Introduction

We all work within complex organizations with diverse interpretations of community engagement. As noted by the Association of Public and Land-Grant Universities (APLU, 2016), community context, institutional mission, and university roles each contribute to how community engagement is enacted, resulting in a "spectrum of engagement issues" to be considered. This leads to a range of activities that can be tracked, monitored, supported, and aligned to reach campus goals for engagement. This "spectrum" can at times complicate the ability to get collective buy-in to support the Elective Carnegie Classification process. We believe that such buy-in is fundamental to the success of this classification process and to the likelihood that community engagement is well aligned with institutional goals to create lasting change.

As cochairs for the Carnegie Reclassification Committee on our campus in 2013–2014, we value the Carnegie process because it is an external lever that supports alignment. It is built upon gathering data, inspiring others to envision new ideas, and leveraging information to support institutional change. We used our talents and the capacities of others across campus to assure that the re-classification process was aligned with other strategic planning efforts, for it is only when alignment occurs across all aspects of institutional work that community engagement leads to transformational change (Association of Public and Land-Grant Universities, 2016; Giles, Sandmann, & Saltmarsh, 2010). As we reflect upon the processes we used to garner campus support for a successful re-classification, we are inspired by jazz as a useful metaphor, and in particular the characteristics of a jazz ensemble.

Like jazz, some of our approach was planned, and some was highly improvisational as we listened and adapted to create a solid performance. Jazz is a window through which we now better understand the approach our campus has taken to align the Carnegie Classification process with other efforts such as accreditation and strategic planning.

What's With Jazz?

Jazz, like community engagement, refers to a spectrum of musical expressions and is challenging to define. A uniquely American musical genre, jazz embraces and balances individual expression of freedom while also being responsible to the functioning and well-being of a larger group (Barrett, 1998). It is partly planned and partly spontaneous; that is, as an ensemble performs, musicians have the opportunity to create their own interpretations in response to the others' performances and whatever else may occur "in the moment."

Improvisation is the defining element of jazz, and musicians see themselves as members of a highly autonomous, interdependent, and mutually enriching unit where creative collaboration is encouraged. Their commitment and passion is predicated on their inherent stake in the success of the performance *and* their ability to take risks. Success is based upon one's own interpretation and ability to improvise. In addition to the formal band leader, improvisation offers a special form of leadership through the act of both "soloing" and "comping" one another (Gold & Hirshfeld, 2005, p. 42; see also Kamoche & Cunha, 2003). Thus, perspectives from jazz informed our work related to community engagement, both in the development of our culture and in the process used to prepare our application for re-classification.

What's Our Context?

We have had numerous opportunities to share the story of community engagement at Indiana University–Purdue University Indianapolis (IUPUI) (e.g., Bringle, Hatcher, & Holland, 2007; Pike, Bringle, & Hatcher, 2014). Our campus is located in the heart of downtown Indianapolis and encompasses 30,000 students, over 7,000 faculty and staff, and 18 degree-granting academic units offering over 300 programs. Throughout its nearly 50-year history, IUPUI has embraced its role as an urban anchor, one that cares deeply about its commitment to community engagement.

Our location matters. To the east, we are in walking distance to state and city government and the economic hub of the city. To the south, we are bordered by museums and cultural organizations. To the west, longtime neighborhood partners and organizations serve as hosts and coeducators for our students. For the purposes of this chapter, it should be noted that to the north, we are bordered by Indiana Avenue, the heart of a vibrant jazz scene, a place the likes of Wes Montgomery, Freddie Hubbard, and David Baker, the internationally renowned musician who founded the acclaimed jazz program at Indiana University, called home. Perhaps it is fair to say that jazz, like community engagement, is in our DNA.

IUPUI has a history of community engagement. The campus was an early adopter of service-learning and strategic campus-community partnerships, and the development and expansion of the Center for Service Learning in the 1990s was a demonstration of IUPUI's commitment to providing students with community-engaged learning experiences and supporting faculty and staff as community-engaged scholars and practitioners. As we prepared for the 2002 accreditation review by the Higher Learning Commission, we redefined our mission to include civic engagement and chose to conduct an elective self-study on civic engagement, laying a strong foundation for our first Carnegie Classification for Community Engagement in 2006.

IUPUI also has a history of planning and assessment. As a part of the self-study, the campus established performance indicators to annually track activities within civic engagement. Across time, nearly every school on campus has documented evidence of community engagement in various forms. In 2013, as a result of a comprehensive strategic planning process, the Office of Community Engagement was created to consolidate campus resources, identify new ways to support campus-community partnerships, improve tracking and monitoring, and tell the story of campus and community impact.

Who Are We?

Preparing for the Carnegie Re-Classification process began in August 2013 when IUPUI Executive Vice Chancellor Nasser Paydar, who now serves as chancellor, asked us (Julie A. Hatcher and Stephen P. Hundley) to cochair our campus application process. He appointed us cochairs of a large committee to complete this task. For the purposes of this chapter, we will often refer to this committee as our "jazz ensemble."

As cochairs we had distinct-yet-complementary roles on campus that were critical to our success. Hatcher's disciplinary expertise is in philanthropic studies, and she serves as the executive director of the Center for Service and Learning. Along with her colleague Bob Bringle, she had been involved in the early conversations at the Carnegie Foundation for the Advancement of Teaching that resulted in the framework for the Elective Classification. As a member of the Elective Carnegie Classification national advisory board, she brought a solid understanding of the field of community engagement. She was well acquainted with the strengths of potential members to convene for the jazz ensemble and identified colleagues well versed in community engagement to bring their expertise and passion to the process. She served as the lead author of the application, with strong support by Kristin Norris, director of assessment in the Office of Community Engagement.

Hundley, now senior adviser to the chancellor for planning and institutional improvement, brought another set of skills and insights to the process. His disciplinary expertise is in organizational leadership, and he had been instrumental in coleading the campus-wide strategic planning process in 2013–2014, resulting in the new IUPUI strategic plan, *Our Commitment to Indiana and Beyond* (IUPUI, 2017). One of the 10 strategic goals calls for IUPUI to "deepen its commitment to community engagement" (p. 9). Hundley was skillful in designing a Carnegie process that would reinforce and align with the strategic plan, recognizing how community engagement serves as its own strategic goal while also integrated into each of the other nine strategic planning goals. In our jazz ensemble, he helped set the tone and cadence for the performance. With Norris's support, we collaboratively crafted agendas for monthly meetings and processes for gathering data to articulate improvements since 2006.

How Did We Feel as the Carnegie Process Unfolded?

Like jazz musicians preparing for performance, we experienced a mixture of feelings as we embarked on our journey: excitement, pride, anticipation, and responsibility. We had a sense that we needed to cultivate dedication to the task and stated early on that upon successful completion we would celebrate with a special gathering of all involved. And, indeed, we did!

We were excited to begin working together as campus leaders on this important process. Together, we benefited from shared knowledge of and passion for IUPUI and had a strong sense of respect for each other's competency and style. This excitement extended to engaging with colleagues and partners who comprised the re-classification application committee. Care and attention was taken to ensure that the jazz ensemble comprised 17 individuals who represented perspectives from all levels and areas of the campus. The committee included deans and other campus-level administrators, faculty with experience in community-engaged projects, professional staff skilled in fostering relationships with our community partners, graduate and undergraduate students, and representatives from community organizations.

We all felt tremendous *pride in our past and present leadership*, which created and sustained commitment to community engagement as a central component of the campus mission. IUPUI has been fortunate to consistently have leaders in the chancellor's cabinet who recognized our responsibility not only to promoting student success and faculty scholarship but also working in a spirit of reciprocity in and with the surrounding community. IUPUI was able to foster *pride in our campus culture* that valued service-learning, community-engaged research and scholarship, and other forms of partnerships with various external organizations. As we gathered evidence, it was apparent that leadership and culture were advanced by investments made to help scale and sustain community engagement at IUPUI, resulting in *pride in our infrastructure to support this work*.

The group also had a sense of anticipation in how the Carnegie Re-Classification process would benefit IUPUI at this juncture of the campus's maturation and development. There was a sense that the work undertaken in support of our application presented an opportunity to *directly contribute to enacting the campus strategic plan.* The collection, reflection, and presentation of our work would help us carry out specific objectives and actions identified in the strategic plan. We also felt the process would permit the campus to *identify strengths to leverage and areas for ongoing improvement.*

The high stakes involved in applying for this prestigious recognition, including demonstrating how we had progressed in our efforts since 2006, manifested in feelings of *responsibility to ourselves and the campus-wide re-classification committee.* This resulted in securing leadership support for our effort, spending time getting to know each other's backgrounds, developing a shared understanding of our committee's approach, and fostering an environment of collaborative effort and mutual respect.

Given the need to reflect a broad array of diverse community engagement work at IUPUI in a relatively constrained application narrative, we also felt a *responsibility to our broader campus and community.* The decentralized nature of IUPUI's structure, coupled with the increase in volume of community engagement work in the past several years, made it challenging for the committee to initially comprehend the diffuse manner in which our work in the community occurs. We were determined to ensure we identified and understood the broad array of work and to use the application process as a means of conveying that work to others.

How Did We Orchestrate the Ensemble?

At the first meeting, time was spent orienting the ensemble members to each other and our task. This involved reviewing the development and significance of the Carnegie Classification, discussing the history of our involvement in community engagement, identifying sources of data that did not exist at the time of the inaugural submission in 2006, and sharing lessons learned from the prior application process.

The committee then agreed upon expectations for its work. This involved discussing our data collection approaches, outlining a time line that included meetings and deliverables, and creating an electronic repository where documents and resources could be shared. We also deliberatively assigned responsibilities of committee members based on sections and subsections of the application narrative (Institutional Culture and Identity, Institutional Commitment, etc.), and we kept our regularly scheduled monthly meetings upbeat and focused by leaning on the expertise of each member to share input from other colleagues across campus. Working group members presented their "work-in-progress" for the full ensemble's reaction and input, and many of these "solo performances" became a source of pride for the rest of the ensemble.

We used the re-classification process to engage approximately 60 stakeholders from across campus in helping collect data, share stories, and enhance understanding of the community engagement work occurring at IUPUI. We involved the dean role as a principal stakeholder to engage first. As academic unit leaders, they helped identify individuals, programs, and partners to consult and include in our application narrative. We asked each dean to complete a survey that was used in 2006 to capture evidence of change related to elements of the application narrative. All of this produced rich information from our colleagues and provided numerous examples from which to choose to demonstrate community engagement's impact at IUPUI. Doing so provided an opportunity to showcase the importance of community engagement as a shared campus value and to educate campus colleagues about the importance of the Carnegie Classification designation.

What Have We Learned About Alignment of Community Engagement?

Some lessons learned from jazz have salience for community engagement work. These include interrupting past habits, embracing errors as a source of learning, distributing tasks with movement toward synchronization, relying on retrospective sense-making, promoting membership in communities of practice, and alternating between soloing and supporting performances (Barrett, 1998; Hatch, 1999).

Our process provided the means to map our engagement efforts against an external, nationally recognized framework. This inspired us to better integrate lessons learned from this process into ongoing and new activities on campus. We are now involved in refreshing the objectives of our strategic plan, including the goal to deepen our community engagement efforts. As part of that process, we are updating performance indicators, incorporating many of the Carnegie Classification framework criteria in those indicators. Such an intentional focus on integrating this work into our planning and improvement efforts is possible because of IUPUI's unique, long-standing cultures focused on both engagement and assessment. We value the Carnegie process as a means to aid our ability to *demonstrate accountability through accreditation and other reporting mechanisms.* Regional and specialized accreditors increasingly make explicit in criteria the need for claims made related to community engagement to be supported by evidence of effectiveness. Work undertaken for the re-classification application helped us establish such evidence.

One challenge is to value both individual and collective performance and to do everything we can to harmonize engagement activities across campus. Campus-level promotion and tenure guidelines; centrally sponsored professional development opportunities; and an overarching coordinating unit, such as IUPUI's Center for Service and Learning, are levers to facilitate this work. It requires that institutions develop the right structures to enhance a supportive performance culture for community engagement. This begins with leaders who are committed to the purposes of engagement and is underscored through strategic directions valuing this work. A focus on engagement is critical to talent recruitment, on-boarding, and advancement processes. As a result of a gap identified through the Carnegie process, we have a three-year Public Scholarship Faculty Learning Community (FLC) initiative. The work of this group has resulted in changes to the campus-level *Promotion and Tenure Guidelines* to now include "public scholarship." In addition, the FLC works to cultivate a supportive culture through a workshop series on public scholarship, an open-access concept paper titled *Public Scholarship & IUPUI*, and mentoring activities.

Investments in professional development, along with rewards, recognition, and resources to support community engagement, further help to establish and reinforce an engaged campus culture. A new campus fellowship program, the Charles R. Bantz Community Fellowship, is now in place to recognize excellence in community-engaged research. Finally, ongoing feedback on performance further reinforces behaviors of faculty, staff, and students. Thus, using data in making decisions, measuring effectiveness, and determining campus priorities helps build a culture of evidence around community engagement.

Concluding Thoughts

Like jazz, community engagement comprises well-meaning professionals who bring a high degree of commitment to the work that they do but who are equally attentive to improvisation as they listen and adapt to others in an effort to reach mutually beneficial goals. Community-engaged scholars enact their passion through their instrument(s) of change (e.g., teaching, research, or service) for the collective good, and such a creative enterprise may seem difficult to orchestrate. Indeed, community engagement may at times appear to be a cacophony of diverse and competing sounds. Yet it can also be an inspiring, vibrant, and soulful expression of the public purposes of higher education. At IUPUI, we value the Carnegie re-classification process for crafting, fine-tuning, and demonstrating our community engagement efforts.

References

Association of Public and Land-Grant Universities. (2016). *The new engagement: Exploring the issues across a spectrum.* Retrieved from http://www.aplu.org/library/the-new-engagement-exploring-the-issues-across-a-spectrum/

Barrett, F. J. (1998). Coda—creativity and improvisation in jazz and organizations: Implications for organizational learning. *Organization Science, 9*(5), 605–622.

Bringle, R. G., Hatcher, J. A., & Holland, B. (2007). Conceptualizing civic engagement: Orchestrating change at a metropolitan university. *Metropolitan Universities, 18*(3), 57–74.

Giles, D. E., Sandmann, L. R., & Saltmarsh, J. (2010). Engagement and the Carnegie classification system. In H. E. Fitzgerald, C. Burack, & S. D. Seifer (Eds.), *Handbook of engaged scholarship: Contemporary landscapes, future directions—Community-campus partnerships* (Vol. 2, pp. 161–176). Lansing, MI: Michigan State University Press.

Gold, M., & Hirshfeld, S. (2005). The behaviors of jazz as a catalyst for strategic renewal and growth. *Journal of Business Strategy, 26*(5), 40–47.

Hatch, M. J. (1999). Exploring the empty spaces of organizing: How improvisational jazz helps redescribe organizational structure. *Organization Studies, 20*(1), 75–100.

IUPUI. (2017). *Our Commitment to Indiana and Beyond.* Retrieved from https://strategicplan.iupui.edu/media/53cd6883-562b-4f80-b9c1-c927c0c4c7fcf/ZEAVVA/StrategicPlanContent/PDF/

Kamoche, K., & Cunha, J. V. D. (2003). Towards a theory of organizational improvisation: Looking beyond the jazz metaphor. *Journal of Management Studies, 40*(8), 2023–2051.

Pike, G. R., Bringle, R. G., & Hatcher, J. A. (2014). Assessing civic engagement at Indiana University-Purdue University Indianapolis. In D. G. Terkla & L. O. Shuler (Eds.), *Assessing community engagement in students* (New Directions for Institutional Research no. 162, pp. 87–97). San Francisco, CA: Jossey-Bass.

Chapter Eleven

PUTTING TOGETHER A TEAM

The "Us" Task

Marisol Morales

On December 4, 2014, I opened my e-mail to find a congratulatory letter from the Carnegie Foundation for the Advancement of Teaching informing us that the University of La Verne had been selected to receive the 2015 Community Engagement Classification as a first-time applicant. I was ecstatic. It was a great success for the University of La Verne, but the rewards of the application came to us even before we received the congratulatory e-mail. The reward came in the diverse teams we were able bring together to institutionalize community engagement in real and tangible ways at the University of La Verne. By bringing together various members of our university community, with a focus on community engagement and the Carnegie Classification, we were able to both leverage our long history and commitment to community engagement and build teams of support that would lead us to achieving the institutional goal of receiving the Carnegie Classification for Community Engagement. In doing so, we are still benefiting from the process and the results.

Setting the Context

When I began my new position as the founding director of the Office of Civic and Community Engagement at the University of La Verne in August 2013, an important requirement of the position was putting together a successful Carnegie Community Engagement Classification application. The University of La Verne was applying for the first time. Although I was excited by the challenge and opportunity to engage in the process, I was also keenly aware that I was a newcomer to the institution and the community. As a newcomer, if I (and we) were to be successful it would be because we formed a strong team of people from across the campus who could pull together the story of engagement of our institution. In my favor, much of the foundational work had been laid prior to my arrival. Teams of individuals who were dedicated to the institution and to community engagement created a space for this process to be collective and desired by our university community. Everyone knew we were applying for the Carnegie Classification, and it made the job of the smaller team that wrote the application easier because everyone was invested in our success, because our success was their success and, ultimately, the University of La Verne's success.

The Carnegie Community Engagement Classification is no small task. The institutional self-study was such an important part of my own learning curve, and it helped the University of La Verne as an institution put a critical and reflective lens to what we were doing and identify what more we wanted to do to further institutionalize community engagement at the university. The ability to pull together teams, in a multistep process—a process that started with the university's strategic plan, which then facilitated the creation of the Office of Civic and Community Engagement and commitment of resources, and culminated with receiving the Carnegie Community Engagement Classification—was critical to making the achievement of the classification something that was achieved by all of us—students, faculty, staff, and community partners. At the University of La Verne, applying for the classification was a collective "us" task because the work belonged to all of us.

126 Years Bold

The University of La Verne was founded in 1891 by the Church of the Brethren. The Church of the Brethren is a Protestant Christian denomination that is recognized as one of the historic peace churches. The church has had a long-standing commitment to peace and justice. The Brethren have been conscientious objectors to military service and as such service to the community has been an important part of Brethren heritage as an alternative to military services. This heritage and background are infused in the University of La Verne's core institutional values. Although the university is no longer formally associated with the Church of the Brethren, the Brethren values and traditions live on in the institution's mission and its four core values—(a) Ethical Reasoning, (b) Diversity and Inclusivity, (c) Lifelong Learning, and (d) Community and Civic Engagement.

The University of La Verne, located in Southern California about 35 miles east of Los Angeles, is a dynamic and diverse institution. It is a comprehensive, doctoral-granting, Hispanic-serving institution with 8,300 students across our 10 Southern California campuses. The university serves 2,800 traditional undergraduate students at the main campus in La Verne, 3,500 nontraditional students (age 23 and above) at 8 regional and online campuses, 240 students at the College of Law, and about 1,800 master's and doctoral students. The student body is diverse, with students of color representing 60% of the student body. Many of the students are first-generation college students coming from a 50-mile radius. The demographics of the institution in many ways represent what most institutions of higher education will come to look like in the coming decades.

Vision 2020

In 2011, the University of La Verne welcomed a new president. Her predecessor had been at the university for 27 years. Our new president was the university's 18th president since its founding in 1891 and the first female president of the university. Her background as an engaged scholar matched the University of La Verne's mission and values and her work ethic and vision for the university brought to the forefront efforts to support community engagement. The excitement of a new president along with the institutional visioning that took place through the strategic plan *Vision 2020* and an interest in sharing who we are as a values-driven institution brought about an opportunity to heighten our visibility, reputation, and prominence.

Although the University of La Verne maintains a long-standing reputation for serving the community, the institutionalization and recognition of community engagement did not take place with a coordinated and centralized vision until the new president's arrival. When I joined the University of La Verne in 2013, the creation of the position of director of civic and community engagement and the pursuit of the Carnegie

Community Engagement classification came as part of a presidential wish list and our university's strategic planning process.

Building the Strategy

In fall 2011, the university began its new strategic planning process, *Vision 2020*, which brought together a diverse group of individuals from across the university to serve on the steering committee. This group developed a bold vision for the University of La Verne through the university's *Vision 2020* strategic planning process, and institutionalizing community engagement was part of that bold effort.

The 21-member Vision 2020 Steering Committee, representing various departments and areas from across the university, worked from fall 2011 through fall 2013. They held four focus groups with faculty, alumni, the Board of Trustees, and students. The final document gave community engagement a prominent role, demonstrated in Strategic Initiatives I and III. In Strategic Initiative I, Achieving Educational Excellence, Objective 1 of Goal 3, Create Centers of Excellence to Meet Evolving National and Global Needs, seeks to "create centers based on areas of institutional strength where faculty teaching, scholarship, and community engagement are brought together with external and community-based initiatives to address regional, national, and global challenges" (University of La Verne, 2013, p. 2). This objective solidified the investment by the University of La Verne in creating the Office of Civic and Community Engagement. In Strategic Initiative III, Heightening Reputation, Visibility, and Prominence, Objective 2 of Goal 1, Achieve National Recognition for Institutional Distinctiveness, seeks to "achieve recognition as a Carnegie Community Engagement campus" (University of La Verne, 2013, p. 4).

Achievement of the Carnegie Classification was very important to the University of La Verne. As Beere, Votruba, and Wells (2011) point out, "The creation of the elective classification sent a clear message that public engagement is neither a passing fad nor unique to a particular college or university. Rather it is highly valued and worthy of recognition in higher education" (p. 25). The timing of the application aligned perfectly with where the University of La Verne was in its institutional transition. It provided a platform to highlight what had been a part of the university's history since 1891. The Carnegie Classification was aligned with who we have been as a mission-driven institution and the role we have played in the local community.

The prominence that community engagement played in the *Vision 2020* document and the direct call for achieving the Carnegie Community

Engagement Classification created an opportunity for us to come together as a campus to engage in the necessary self-study and achieve the goal. In addition, the goals of that vision were substantiated with a dedication of resources to create the Office of Civic and Community Engagement and to hire a director. As Holland (1997) points out, the creation of service-learning centers or community engagement offices to provide leadership and assistance indicates an institutional commitment and expectation of participation by faculty, students, and community partners. Applying for the Carnegie Classification and dedicating resources toward the creation of the office demonstrated that the University of La Verne was invested and began to own its identity as an engaged campus.

Fertile Ground: Preparing the Institution to Pursue Carnegie

The initial team that brought the vision of successful achievement of the Carnegie Community Engagement Classification began long before I arrived at the University of La Verne. This initial group helped set the stage for the creation of the Office of Civic and Community Engagement, and many of the Vision 2020 Steering Committee members served on the search committee for the position I now hold, director of civic and community engagement. They knew that in order to achieve the Carnegie Classification they would need to hire someone to spearhead the effort of institutionalizing community engagement on campus and drive the development of a successful application. I was able to walk into a supportive atmosphere of faculty, staff, and community members because of the fertile ground that had been cultivated through our university values, a supportive and knowledgeable community-engaged president, and a strategic planning committee that actively listened to members of the university community and prominently included community engagement in its bold vision for the university. The members of this original steering committee continue to serve as allies in the community engagement efforts of the Office of Civic and Community Engagement.

As the facilitator and primary writer of the Carnegie Community Engagement Classification proposal and a newcomer to both California and the University of La Verne, I knew that successful achievement would only come if we built upon the goodwill toward the Carnegie Classification initiated by the Vision 2020 Steering Committee. To this end we continued viewing this as a collective effort. As a first-time classification applicant, the university did not have anyone who had a background on the classification application, and even though I came from another institution that did have the Carnegie Classification, my role there did not entail facilitating or writing the application. This endeavor would be new to all of us, but it provided an opportunity to engage in relationship-building, process analysis, and data collection in order to provide the most comprehensive self-study that we, as an institution, had attempted around community engagement. The task was both daunting and exciting. There were times when I questioned whether or not we were ready, but the makeup of the writing team and the support from the members of the University of La Verne community helped to dismiss the negative thoughts and make the case for why the University of La Verne was worthy of the Carnegie Classification. The team was crucial to our success. This was not a one-person endeavor.

Building Our Writing Team

Although the primary motivation for the institution lay in achieving national recognition for its community engagement efforts, the benefit for me as a newcomer was that the application provided me with an opportunity to learn the landscape of community engagement at the University of La Verne in a relatively short amount of time. The Carnegie Classification served as a platform for the Office of Civic and Community Engagement to build intentional, asset-based, and transformative community engagement at the University of La Verne that would be responsive to the university's diverse student body and to do so with a bold vision. With this in mind, the writing team was composed of the story keepers, the midways, and the newbies. The story keepers were individuals who had been at the University of La Verne for several decades and had experienced the transitions of the institution over decades. These individuals held the historical memory and provided valuable information as we were developing the application. The midways were those individuals who had been at the university five to seven years and held good working knowledge of data and the ins and outs of the university. They knew who to ask and where to find the data. The newbies were the recent arrivals to the University of La Verne. We had been at the institution less than a year, but we came from other institutions and brought new insights and understanding of community engagement work. The benefit of having this institutional intergenerational team was that we were able to merge insights, experience, and vision to engage in a self-study that brought forth both the richness of the institution's past efforts and the possibilities of what was to come.

The writing team was composed of a total of six individuals. We divided the team between the writers of the document and the reviewers. This multilayered approach allowed the writers to move sections of the application through to review as we finished writing or collecting the data for the other sections. We would then go back to include the feedback we received from the reviewers. The writers were the director of civic and community engagement, the associate provost, the university chaplain, and the assistant dean of the College of Arts and Sciences. The reviewers were the director of the La Verne Experience and the director of the Center for Faculty Excellence. The newbies were myself and the associate provost; the midways were the assistant dean of the College of Arts and Sciences and the director of the Center for the Advancement of Faculty Excellence; and the story keepers were the director of the La Verne Experience, who had been at the University of La Verne for 30 years, and the university chaplain, who had been with the university for 15 years. Both are also alumni of the University of La Verne. This rich and diverse team took on the challenge and engaged in a process that incorporated insights gained through community forums by taking anecdotal stories of engagement to piece together the puzzle of the scope of institutional outreach as well as sorting through data about classes and students. We reviewed course syllabi; examined financial and university documents; and studied student, alumni, faculty, and staff stories to get the most comprehensive understanding of our engagement efforts to include in our Carnegie application.

In Reflection

The payoff of the intense work and time that went into pulling together the Carnegie application was knowing that we had an important story to share and that the time it took to put together a successful application was an investment in the future of community engagement at the University of La Verne. The Carnegie application served as a roadmap, and the team that pulled it off was able to begin that journey together. Although the Office of Civic and Community Engagement was the lead and took on the primary role of writing and submitting the application, the teams that came from across the university both in the initial visioning and goal of pursuing the Carnegie Classification and creating the Office of Civic and Community Engagement and the team that coalesced to write the application were essential in making the goal become a reality. The pursuit of common goals, institutionalizing community engagement at the University of

La Verne and achieving the Carnegie Classification, were what brought together these strong and dynamic teams who had the support of their president. It was an "us" task from the beginning and it continues to be as we further institutionalize community engagement at the University of La Verne and do so with a vision toward community assets, partnerships, and critical engagement.

References

Beere, C. A., Votruba, J. C., & Wells, G. W. (2011). *Becoming an engaged campus: A practical guide for institutionalizing public engagement.* San Francisco, CA: Jossey-Bass.

Holland, B. A. (1997). Analyzing institutional commitment to service: A model of key organizational factors. *Michigan Journal of Community Service Learning, 4*(1), 30–41.

University of La Verne. (2013). *Vision 2020.* La Verne, CA: 2020 Strategic Vision Steering Committee.

Chapter Twelve

A NEVER-ENDING
JOURNEY, BUT AT
LEAST THERE'S
A ROADMAP

Capitalizing on Achieving the Classification and Looking Ahead to Re-Classification

Brenda Marsteller Kowalewski

I [Brenda] was sitting in the Denver airport waiting for my connecting flight to return home to Ogden, Utah, when I received the e-mail that my institution, Weber State University (WSU), earned the 2008 Carnegie Community Engagement Classification. Initially, I couldn't believe it! I was stunned! Thrilled! Elated, really! All that hard work had paid off. Time to kick back, celebrate and brag a bit . . . or so we originally thought.

Having been through both classification (2008) and re-classification (2015), I've learned that the Carnegie Community Engagement Classification is not meant to sit on a shelf like a stagnant glass-engraved award whose best use is collecting dust. It is not meant to be stagnant.

The Carnegie Community Engagement Classification is a dynamic process with two distinct parts, both of which should be leveraged to advance community engagement work on our campuses. Part one in the process is the act of applying for the classification, which offers an opportunity to leverage the documentation framework, as well as the process of completing it, to further institutionalize community engagement on our campuses. Part two in the process is the act of actually earning the classification, which offers an opportunity to leverage the recognition that accompanies the classification. Both parts in this process build on each other, making it rather cyclical in nature. Ultimately, this process can be used to build toward your ideal community-engaged campus.

2008 Classification

When the provost of Weber State University proposed we apply for this new Elective Classification for Community Engagement in 2008, he did so with the intent of using the process to help us build the infrastructure of our very new center responsible for promoting community engagement on campus. I wasn't aware of his intentions at the time. However, as it turns out, this transformation style of leadership that is so essential for leading engaged institutions (Sandmann & Plater, 2009) was critical for me as the principal writer and facilitator of the application, because it allowed me to leverage the application process as a tool for furthering our community engagement work.

Part One: Application Process—Leveraging the Documentation Framework as a Roadmap

I was a half-time center director and half-time faculty member who had been tasked with applying for the Elective Classification just months after our Center for Community Engaged Learning (CCEL) had been formally established on campus. I recall reading all the questions in the documentation framework and feeling overwhelmed by the high bar it set. I felt like it was describing the infrastructure necessary to build the ideal community engagement center on the ideal community-engaged campus. Earning this classification felt like a tall order for such a young center, even though our university has been engaged with the community from its inception over 100 years ago. But the expectation had been set by the administration so it was time to double down. One of the first things I did was attend a workshop on the classification delivered by John Saltmarsh. Afterward, I naively asked him if my institution had to say yes to every question in the documentation framework. He basically said, ideally community-engaged institutions should be doing all of these things. He followed up by saying, "Just don't plan on earning the classification the first time you apply." I went back to my campus even more motivated to build the necessary infrastructure within the new center so we could confidently mark yes to everything on the application. But I told my president and provost we should be prepared not to earn the classification the first time we applied.

From that point forward, the documentation framework became the roadmap. In approximately one year, whatever was missing in our infrastructure was built, enabling us to mark a solid yes to every question on the classification application. But let me be clear, this process was far more intentional and strategic than simply checking boxes on an application. We leveraged the weight of this external Carnegie Classification and the desire of the provost to earn it to get different parts of campus to work with us. And we used the application process to build missing pieces of the infrastructure across campus. For example, the registrar's office agreed to note excellence in community engagement on students' transcripts. A process for formally designating CEL courses was developed, employed, and reflected in the class schedule so students could find these courses more easily. A newly hired center employee was tasked with figuring out an existing underutilized software system for tracking volunteer hours, which became the central tracking system of community engagement for the university. Feedback loops in the form of annual surveys were developed and administered for all stakeholder groups served, including community partners, faculty, staff, and students. Space to highlight community-engaged learning pedagogies and research was added to the standardized form faculty complete as part of the rank and tenure process. And so it went. Whatever the documentation framework called for, we put into place or formalized what was once informally happening.

The documentation framework served as a roadmap in another way as well. I've noticed that each time we've completed the application process in both 2008 and 2015, the framework always includes an optional question or two. In 2008, for example, the framework had an optional question about how our institution recognized community-engaged work in the rank and tenure process. This optional question was a seed being planted in the "brains" of institutions. It was basically saying, if you haven't thought about this yet, you need to. If you have thought about this, tell us about it and evaluate where you can improve it. This optional question in 2008 became a required question in 2015. In this way, the framework serves as a roadmap for where your institution should be heading and making progress toward over the next 10 years, which is exactly when you will be reapplying for the classification. In other words, the documentation framework itself tells you where the field is going and what the expectations are for your institution to keep pace in facilitating high-quality community-engaged work.

The application process also provided a fabulous opportunity to self-assess on various criteria indicating institutionalization of community engagement at WSU. However, self-assessment wasn't the key outcome we were looking for because we had already engaged in self-assessment using Holland's (1997) tool a few years prior. We were looking for a tool that could be leveraged to create change. That is exactly what the Carnegie Community Engagement Classification documentation framework had to offer our campus that the Holland (1997) tool could not. The classification was an external impetus that could be leveraged to convince others on campus to create the necessary changes to become the institution we wanted to be. Why? Because, in order to earn the recognition, it isn't enough to self-assess. Campuses have to act on what they learn from the assessment. They have to get to the "yes" on the documentation framework.

Much like the reports from the institutions that had earned the classification in 2006 (Driscoll, 2009), Weber State was motivated by the application process. We were motivated to make immediate changes and once we saw that was possible, we were motivated to continue to make changes to improve upon the initial strides made in this first application round. Holland (2009) notes that "the data reported by institutional applicants provide an interesting portrait of organizational change in action" (p. 86). For WSU, these changes were in building a solid infrastructure upon which to establish our "ideal" community-engaged campus.

Part Two: Earning the Classification—Leveraging the Recognition

After earning the classification in 2008, we started including it in printed materials and on websites. It certainly gave our president and administration a point of pride to boast about. However, we quickly came to realize having earned the classification was so much more than a talking point or feather in our cap. A momentum had been created during the application process that was now being fueled by having actually earned the classification. We began to harness the power of that momentum to help us become the institution we wanted to be by the time we were going to apply for the classification again. It became crystal clear that earning the classification was not an end goal; it was a stepping-stone in our community engagement journey.

We began to use the classification as a reaffirmation of who we are as an institution and how important community is to our mission and purpose. For example, shortly after earning the classification, WSU engaged in a process of revising our university mission and vision. In that process, we identified three core themes—access, learning, and community. With this change, we formally owned our long history of creating and nurturing strong ties to the community. In a way, earning the classification gave us permission to tout our commitment to the community more overtly than perhaps we had in the past. This became evident in the way we began orienting new faculty to the university, for example. After the classification, orientation has always been done with a full understanding that WSU is Carnegie classified for community engagement. We tell faculty that this is who we are and what we do at Weber State University and then we proceed to acquaint them with all the resources they have at their fingertips to employ community-engaged learning in their courses. This message has been delivered faithfully every year since having earned the classification in 2008.

Earning the classification has facilitated the "alignment of commitment, mission, public declaration, resources, policies and procedures (including recognition of civic engagement as proper faculty work), planning, measurable goals, and accountability" (Sandmann & Plater, 2009, p. 22). It set in motion organizational change. All units and divisions on campus became responsible for articulating how their work aligns with the university's core themes. So all units and divisions began to highlight and promote the work they were doing with the community more intentionally than in the past. Strategic plans for each division included goals related to the core theme—community. Annual reports included highlights of work done with and for the community. Recognition of community-engaged faculty was formalized in letters submitted to promotion and tenure files. For example, as director of the Center for Community Engaged Learning at the time, I was referencing the Carnegie Community Engagement Classification in every letter I was writing for a community-engaged faculty member's promotion and tenure file—for example, "As an institution that has earned the Carnegie Community Engagement Classification, retaining faculty members, like Dr. So-and-so, who teach their students through community-engaged learning techniques and turn it into community-engaged scholarship, is essential." Without having earned the classification, these organizational changes may have never occurred or at best developed more slowly.

We also found the classification created some stability for our institution when facing a presidential transition. The classification has the power to help diffuse the idea of community engagement and sustain it from administration to administration. As Holland (2009) notes, "Institutionalization can be achieved or destroyed overnight by changes in the occupants of key administrative roles" (p. 89). We found the classification guards against instability if leveraged. In 2012, our long-serving and dedicated community-engaged president announced she was stepping down. I was asked to serve on the presidential search committee. It became clear immediately that I was not the only person in the room talking about the importance of finding a president committed to the community to help us maintain our classification. In fact, it was remarkable to see how many candidates referenced WSU's community classification during the interview process. The classification became a badge that both the search committee and the candidates had no choice but to acknowledge and honor.

Once our new president was selected, he asked me about community engagement. What an opportunity to leverage the classification once again. I shared with him the feedback we received from the Carnegie Foundation regarding our shortcomings in the 2008 application process—recognizing community engagement in the promotion and tenure processes and creating better assessment and systematic tracking mechanisms. He quickly understood that in order to keep our classification in the future, we needed to make changes in these two areas. Additionally, he knew that better data would help him tell WSU students' stories more fully, an asset when embarking on a capital campaign, which the institution was on the verge of doing. Resources were allocated for a more robust tracking system and the provost challenged the dean of the College of Social and Behavioral Sciences to revise the college tenure document to recognize community-engaged work in teaching, scholarship, and service, with the expectation that this tenure document would become a model for other colleges to follow. The wheels of more organizational change were set in motion.

Earning the classification in 2008 had an external impact as well. This impact seemed to develop more slowly than the internal impacts and was far less intentional or strategic. The news of having earned the classification was quietly shared with partnering community organizations without much fanfare. This began to raise awareness about what the university was doing in the community. I can't say we intentionally leveraged the classification in 2008 to create this increase in awareness, but earning the classification offered an opportunity to deepen, strengthen, and expand partnerships that we leveraged in the 2015 round. In 2008, our surrounding city of Ogden was becoming more aware and excited about all the work the university was doing in the community and began to think about how to leverage it to help them achieve their goal of becoming a college town. At this point in our Carnegie Community Engagement journey, our city partners were thinking more about leveraging the earned classification with audiences external to the university than we were.

2015 Re-Classification

After having earned the classification in 2008, the pressure was on to re-classify in 2015. We had to demonstrate what we had actually improved or changed from 2008 to 2015. I remember feeling the weight of that responsibility and asking myself how much change is enough to maintain the classification. I knew we had been doing good work and making progress toward the ideal type laid out in the documentation framework, our roadmap, but we weren't there yet. We were continuing to strive and had made improvements. I just didn't know if it was enough. Additionally, I didn't know if the process I used for writing the application in 2008 was going to be the best process for telling this story of change. The university's formal ownership and commitment to community engagement had evolved on campus well beyond the walls of the Center for Community Engaged Learning. Who did I need in the application process to help tell this story? Ultimately, I decided to employ a completely different process to complete the application in 2015 than I had employed in 2008. It was the best decision I could have possibly made.

Part Three: Application Process—Leveraging an Inclusive Process for Applying

An inclusive approach to completing the 2015 application mobilized the campus and community to participate in the process of reapplying for the classification. Comparatively, in 2008, I drove the application process and asked for help from individuals along the way as needed. Lots of people participated in the application process but they did so in their silos. They provided the information or assistance I requested without understanding where and how that information or assistance fit into the larger application and, therefore, the larger Weber State community engagement story. In 2015, the process was completely different. I assembled a large, 30-person task force that included representatives from all stakeholder groups: students, faculty, staff, administrators, and community partners. The group met in its entirety periodically and in subcommittees more frequently throughout the application year. A clear sense of purpose, knowledge of the overall documentation framework, and an articulated process for completing the application was supported by all task force members. They understood their roles and purpose on the task force and the roles and responsibilities of other task force members. The task of telling WSU's community-engaged story in the Carnegie Community Engagement Re-Classification application was embraced by the task force as a collective. They were thoughtful about how they could support and assist each other in completing their assigned sections. There was true teamwork to complete the application, which led to teamwork to advance WSU's community engagement work more generally.

Knowing that it was going to be especially important to tell our story of change in the two areas in which we fell short in 2008, a subcommittee was created for each of those areas. A promotion and tenure subcommittee consisting of senior faculty members with representation from each of the seven colleges in the university was assembled. This committee was tasked with the responsibility for writing the promotion and tenure section of the application, which they did. But what ended up happening was far more important than their writing of the application. The collective approach to writing the application allowed this group to work as a team to continue to advance the work that had already begun in modifying college tenure documents. They had questions about how faculty perceived, valued, and rated community-engaged work in the promotion and tenure process, which led to the group designing and completing a research project. The data from the research informed a proposal the group wrote to the Faculty Senate to consider changing the promotion guidelines to be more consistent with the revised college tenure documents. So, although writing the Carnegie application collectively, this team of senior faculty members was able to see what still needed to be done to better recognize and reward community-engaged faculty in the promotion and tenure process, which led them to take action.

Another subcommittee on assessment and tracking, again a noted shortcoming in 2008, was developed. Membership consisted of individuals responsible for data and assessment in academic matters, student affairs, and institutional research more generally. The subcommittee's charge was to respond to the assessment and tracking sections of the application, and, like the promotion and tenure subcommittee, this subcommittee was spurred to action. Collectively, the group began to see the need for aligning the data collection efforts our institution uses for reporting in the Carnegie Community Engagement Classification application to the data collection efforts we use in the accreditation process. Although the alignment of these processes could not occur during the year we were writing the re-classification application, the wheels were set in motion by the team to begin aligning metrics and tools to bring more parity into data collection for re-classification and accreditation while also streamlining the process. Again, the application process itself, when pursued as a collective, inclusive process, was used to create institutional change.

A third subcommittee was formed to complete the community partnership grid for that section of the application. This community partnership committee was cochaired with a community partner from the city of Ogden. Committee membership was evenly split between university stakeholders and community partners. I marveled at the application writing process itself because community partners, faculty, staff, and students were stepping up to take the lead on writing about different partnerships that were being highlighted on the grid. The commitment to and excitement for the work was incredible. The inclusive approach to writing the application afforded all members of the subcommittee, but especially community partners, a front row seat to all the different activities the university was involved in with the community. The scope and depth of university community partnerships was being exposed to them for the first time. There was a genuine excitement about the amazing work that was taking place and an equally genuine disappointment that these stories were not more prevalent in the community. This was a striking wake up call for me and other university folks. It showed us that we had successfully told our story to our internal campus community since earning the classification in 2008. We had community as a core theme and were actively telling our stories in annual reports and highlighting community-engaged students in recruitment materials. But we weren't telling these stories to our community partners. And so, once again, the application process inspired action. The committee became the advocates for telling community engagement stories to external audiences. One of the first action items for this group after reapplication was a public celebration for having earned the classification again in 2015—but more on that later.

In addition to leveraging the writing process to advance our community-engaged work, the documentation framework in 2015 continued to serve as a roadmap. The optional question in the framework for 2015 had to do with how the institution is utilizing community engagement to better serve historically underrepresented students in higher education.

Quite frankly, WSU was not intentionally employing community-engaged learning very well to serve underrepresented students. It was occurring by happenstance, but it certainly was not intentional. This question on the documentation framework inspired the CCEL to develop a position to focus on exactly this—intentionally engaging more underrepresented students in the community to increase their success at WSU. The documentation framework tells you where the field is going. Our goal is to be one of the top-notch community-engaged campuses in the country, which means we need to keep pace with the field. Our roadmap is clear. We need to figure out how to better serve underrepresented students via community-engaged learning and develop measures to assess how well we are doing it before the next application round.

Part Four: Earning the Classification—Leveraging Ownership of the Recognition

I shouldn't have been surprised that employing a different process for writing the application would result in a different reaction to earning it, but I was. The difference was dramatic. Ownership of the classification expanded within and beyond the university. Outside the university, joint ownership of the classification between the university and the community was publicly named and celebrated. Within the university, responsibility for maintaining WSU's Carnegie Community Engagement Classification moved from the Center for Community Engaged Learning to the Provost Office, giving it a broader university platform. Both of these renegotiated definitions of *classification ownership* are moving WSU another step closer to the community-engaged university we are striving to become before the next application round in 2025.

The inclusive, collaborative approach to writing the application in 2015 was mainly used to increase ownership of the process for applying for re-classification. The logic was that everyone was responsible for telling the story of progress and change, so everyone owned the story. What this really meant was everyone owned the recognition that accompanies having earned the re-classification. Our community partners owned the classification as much as the university did. It became clear that WSU hadn't earned re-classification. We, the university and our community, had earned the Carnegie Community Engagement Classification. This was a distinctly different and incredibly more refreshing reaction to earning the classification than in 2008.

As part of the work of the community partner subcommittee, a large public celebration occurred in February of 2015 to recognize a successful reapplication process. The city of Ogden and WSU took the lead in planning and funding the event, which was intentionally designed to celebrate a joint classification for the university and the community. We celebrated and acknowledged the fact that the university could have never achieved such recognition without the partnership of the city and surrounding community. Longtime community partners who had a relationship with WSU of 50 years or more were honored with granite "Bedrock Awards." In addition, Ogden gave WSU's CCEL the "keys to their community" and invited other cities and towns that WSU serves to do the same. The evening was jubilant and generated increased awareness and positive energy for developing deeper, stronger, and more numerous university community partnerships.

The external announcement and ownership of the re-classification shouldn't be underestimated. Community partners' awareness of the university as a resource expanded that evening. Their thinking about what the university has to offer them forever changed. As a result, we've noticed an increase in what Sandmann, Thornton, and Jaeger (2009) call community-to-university inbound programs—partners initiating projects rather than waiting for the university to come to them with an offer to help. This couldn't be more evident than in our Research Extension of the CCEL, which has more community-based research requests from partners now than ever before. The public celebration of the re-classification also helped the university expand its role to include more convener/facilitator activities than ever before. For example, WSU is acting as a convener for the Ogden Civic Action Network (OgdenCAN), which includes seven anchor institutions, nonprofit organizations, local businesses, and Ogden residents to address concerns related to health, education, and housing in a particular Ogden neighborhood. The Carnegie Community Engagement Classification has become an important part of the conversation with the network members to help them understand why the university would play this facilitator/convener role. The classification legitimizes the university's commitment to playing a central role in discovering transdisciplinary community solutions. The classification is helping us as an institution fulfill a role we wish to play in our community.

Ownership of the classification on campus has also expanded. All the areas of campus that participated in writing the application now understand how their areas contribute to WSU earning the classification. They own their part and are proud to do so. In 2016, we also moved the responsibility of maintaining the classification from the Center for Community Engaged Learning to the Provost Office. The move coincided with a change in my role at the institution from CCEL director to associate provost for high-impact programs and faculty development. Moving the responsibility for the classification to the Provost Office actually does two things: it puts this accreditation-like process in the same office responsible for accreditation, and it puts the responsibility for coordinating, facilitating, and maintaining the classification in an office that is responsible for collaborating with all entities across campus. The move was informed, at least in part, by the work of the subcommittee on assessment and tracking that wrote those parts of the application in 2015. This committee recommended aligning the Carnegie application process with the accreditation process. This seemed like a natural way to begin to accomplish this goal. Linking engagement with accreditation is an opportunity afforded to institutions that have earned the classification. At WSU, we continue to work to align the accreditation metrics associated with the community core theme to the metrics used in the Carnegie Community Engagement Classification.

It's All About the Process

I am so grateful for the process in which my institution has been engaged since 2007 when the provost first mentioned applying for the new Carnegie Community Engagement Classification. It has set us on a course for becoming the community-engaged campus we want to be. In the process we have learned how well we have institutionalized community engagement, what we need to do to improve it, and how we can leverage both the process of applying and actually earning the classification to advance our work.

I believe the Carnegie Community Engagement Classification offers each institution applying for it, and/or earning it, an opportunity to engage in a transformative process—a process that continues from application cycle to application cycle. If an institution is really going to leverage the classification, it must engage in the process with an openness, willingness, and desire to be transformed as an institution. Those who do so are handsomely rewarded with organizational and cultural changes that better serve the students, staff, faculty, and community.

I encourage you to follow the roadmap. Embrace the process. Then, like every other institution that has received the classification to date, your institution won't receive an award or plaque in the mail. Rather, you'll earn the opportunity to engage in an ongoing improvement process that will help you build the community-engaged institution you so desire. For WSU, this process is a gift that just keeps giving.

References

Driscoll, A. (2009). Carnegie's new community engagement classification: Affirming higher education's role in community. *New Directions for Higher Education*, no. 147, 5–12.

Holland, B. A. (1997). Analyzing institutional commitment to service: A model of key organizational factors. *Michigan Journal of Community Service Learning*, 4(1), 30–41.

Holland, B. A. (2009). Will it last?: Evidence of institutionalization at Carnegie classified community engagement institutions. *New Directions for Higher Education*, no. 147, 85–98.

Sandmann, L. R., & Plater, W. M. (2009). Leading the engaged institution. *New Directions for Higher Education*, no. 147, 13–24.

Sandmann, L. R., Thornton, C. H., & Jaeger, A. J. (2009). The first wave of community-engaged institutions. *New Directions for Higher Education*, no. 147, 99–104.

Chapter Thirteen

WHERE ARE YOU GOING? WHERE HAVE YOU BEEN?

How a Campus Rethought Its Community Engagement Agenda After a Failed Carnegie Attempt

Monica Kowal

Introduction

This chapter was written in the hopes that it would provide both solace and guidance to universities and colleges that have attempted but failed to receive the Carnegie Foundation's Elective Community Engagement Classification. By policy, the "administrative partner" for the foundation does not reveal the names of campuses that fail to receive the designation; however, after a brief discussion with the editors of this volume and members of my institution's executive leadership team (i.e., the president and associate provost), we felt that there would be significant value in divulging our journey from this failed attempt in 2015 to our new attempt in 2020.

When I was chosen to lead the self-study process for the University of New Mexico's (UNM's) 2015 application, the institution had maintained an impressive record of outreach and engagement initiatives; however, I and my team found it increasingly difficult to discern where and to whom we should go to begin our self-assessment process. My first and greatest challenge—more than identifying members of a steering committee or finding adequate resources for the endeavor—was building a historical narrative around UNM's engagement efforts up to that point. The more I began to rally support, the more I learned about previous efforts to qualify and quantify past engagement efforts. There were rumors of an engaged faculty network, tales of a fairly substantial engagement summit, phantom reports that some person in some department possessed. As I had only been at my institution for three years, cobbling together an institutional memoir was frustrating. No one could remember who did what or what the outcomes were for all these past initiatives. It was clear that we were, essentially, going to have to start from scratch.

Researcher as Instrument

I began my career at UNM teaching as a term lecturer in the English department, filling a role as an instructor for freshman composition and technical writing classes. Prior to this, I had been teaching in a local high school (at which I was also the service-learning coordinator) and working on my doctorate in curriculum and instruction. My background as a service-learning (SL) coordinator and my doctoral studies in SL curriculum and program design led me to ask a logical question when I came to UNM: Can I incorporate SL into my courses? I was told by a department administrator that I could not compel students to do work off campus as part of the course requirements. I could suggest it, but it could not be held against them if they did not participate. It was clear that the person offering me these suggestions was operating under the definition of *community service* as opposed to *SL*, so my first task was to suss out whether the university had any kind of language or guidelines that more clearly defined *SL*. (It is also worth noting that I am the type of person who views "no" as an opportunity to forge a path to "yes.") As expected, I found no explicit rule stating that SL *could not* be used as a teaching strategy or as part of a course objective or assessment. In fact, during my search I discovered that the university had a Research Service-Learning Program (RSLP) and a Community Engagement Center (CEC).

The CEC was formed in 2000 and operated under the auspices of the associate vice president of student affairs with a director, two program coordinators, and one administrative assistant. The program operated several AmeriCorps-funded programs, including the UNM Service Corps, Tribal Service Corps, and Teacher Service Corps. The RSLP was founded in 2006 and housed in University College, an academic unit that operated the institution's freshman learning communities, a bachelor of liberal arts program, and other initiatives. The strength of the CEC and RSLP was that both were very community-centric, focused on developing long-term, collaborative relationships based on community-identified needs. The weakness was that neither unit focused on supporting faculty in the development of community-based learning courses nor working with administration to create university-wide guidelines or policies around SL. Neither unit systematically tracked or monitored the impact of their relationships with community partners, nor did they regularly collect data on how SL or community-based courses and programs impacted student success.

I spent my first year at UNM refining and improving my own curriculum, incorporating SL into my technical and professional writing courses, and finishing my dissertation. Before long, I was being asked to talk about SL at daylong workshops and seminars hosted by our Center for Teaching and Learning. Some faculty began asking me how they might get involved in doing this type of work, and others said they were already doing something similar to SL but desired more guidance and support. I began working with the director of the RSLP to create criteria for SL or community-based research classes and distributed those guidelines across campus. The director of the RSLP also said he had been working with the registrar's office to have courses designated as SL or community-based research courses. Small steps toward large change were occurring.

In the fall of 2012, I was invited to participate in the Emerging Engagement Scholars Workshop at the Engagement Scholarship Consortium Conference in Alabama. It was during this experience that I was first introduced to the concept of the *engaged scholar* and the Carnegie Foundation's Elective Classification process. It was also the first time I had heard university leaders—presidents, provosts, and chancellors— talk about their *engaged campus* agendas and their quest for the Carnegie designation. I also attended a talk by Amy Driscoll on the first round of Carnegie-classified institutions that were now applying for re-classification. It occurred to me that this might be something that my institution could strive to attain. We had lots of engaged teaching, both large-scale and small-scale community-engaged research partnerships, and we had a plethora of outreach programs. There was a significant foundation, save for a few key elements. During the conference, one theme emerged from all of the sessions I attended: the revision of faculty tenure and promotion policies to be more inclusive of community-engaged scholarship was the tipping point for a shift in campus culture around community engagement. As a newly minted PhD, I could not fathom how or where to begin this conversation; however, I did know that a good place to start was with engaging those faculty, staff, and administrators who I knew were already doing engaged work.

The fall of 2012 also marked the inaugural year for a new UNM president, a native son who was returning to his alma mater after serving as provost at Kent State University. As part of his inauguration week, a forum was presented highlighting community-based work done by university faculty with representation from our Center for Educational Policy Research (CEPR) and the Southwest Hispanic Research Institute (SHRI), as well as the Chicano studies, computer science, and architecture and planning departments. Each faculty member presented work that was clearly community engaged. But when I asked whether any of them included this work as scholarship in their tenure portfolios, their collective silence spoke volumes. It was at this point that—despite my very tenuous and low-level position on campus—I committed myself to figuring out how to become a change agent for community engagement at my university, and I would begin by convincing UNM that they needed to try for the Carnegie designation in 2015.

Endeavoring to Attain the 2015 Carnegie Designation

New Mexico is a state rich in history and culture, but more than 20% of our residents live in poverty, and our unemployment rate is nearly 7% (in some counties that rate reaches well above 20%). The economy in our state is buoyed by the service industry, defense (we have two national scientific laboratories and four military bases), local and federal government, health care, and—to a large extent—oil and gas, which creates an irregular and inconsistent outlook for both the public and private sectors. As both a Carnegie-classified "very high research" institution and a Hispanic-serving institute (HSI), UNM is in a unique position to leverage its leadership potential by promoting and celebrating the community engagement initiatives undertaken by students, faculty, and staff. As New Mexico's flagship public university, UNM plays an essential role in the vitality and sustainability of our state. Our research, teaching, and learning impacts the well-being of thousands of New Mexicans. Still, it is not unusual for an institution such as ours—deeply anchored in the context and culture of its host city and state—to imagine that our influence and impact on our surrounding communities is greater than it is. Like many institutions, we struggle with defining *community*. We also often confuse *economic development* with *community engagement*, a distinction that we in the community engagement field draw upon on a regular basis but continue to emphasize that, although the focal points of these two areas might be the same, our means to those ends—capacity building, innovation, addressing social justice issues, decreasing socioeconomic disparities, and the like— are unique.

With all of these issues in mind, we set out to construct UNM's narrative of engagement. A colleague and mentor of mine was serving as an administrative fellow in the president's office. She was an SL practitioner in the College of Education and proved to be a formidable connection to key administrators in the Provost's Office. Once I engaged my colleague as an ally of this process, the next several weeks were spent working with her and various administrators to assemble a steering committee that would work to lead the self-study process. In addition to the directors of the CEC and the RSLP, we pulled together faculty from various departments who were willing to carve a path for data collection. In addition to assembling this ad hoc team, I was fortunate enough to find a champion in Virginia Scharff, a distinguished professor of history and the newly appointed associate provost for faculty development, whose advocacy within Scholes Hall (our administrative building) gave the Carnegie project the much-needed credence and momentum to propel us to the finish line. Still, with only 5 months to conduct the self-study on a campus of 15 academic units (colleges, schools, and branch campuses), more than 100 departments, more than 4,000 faculty, and more than 35,000 students, that finish line loomed large.

We decided to conduct the data collection in phases: phase one would focus on communicating the project to the larger campus community and briefing as many people as possible on the information we were seeking. We presented to the Deans' Council, the Faculty Senate, the Health Sciences Center's administrative team, department chairs, directors, to smaller groups within the schools and colleges around campus, and to anyone else who would listen. Phase two included the creation of a fairly simple survey that pared down the criteria from the Carnegie application. We distributed it via the campus electronic mailing service and asked deans, chairs, and directors to assign at least one person to serve as the liaison for the data collection process. Once the responses started to roll in, it became clear that, as the sole operational leader of the process, I was going to need some help. The dean of our graduate studies program agreed to fund two graduate research assistant positions, and with their help we began phase three, which involved creating a plan for following up with units that did not respond to the survey or to fill in gaps in their survey responses.

Data were collected between November 2013 and March 2014. Both the president's and provost's offices issued a campus-wide call to participate. Two surveys were distributed to deans, chairs, and program directors. Units also had the option of submitting their program's annual report or arranging for a member of the steering committee to come and interview directly them about their program. More than 30 units across campus and from branch campuses self-reported community engagement initiatives ranging from course-based practices to major research partnerships. Additionally, the steering committee conducted research to find examples from schools, colleges, and programs that did not self-report but that were believed to have courses, outreach programs, and partnerships that fit the parameters of the data collection process. The actual writing of the application occurred in the final month leading up to Carnegie's deadline. After vetting the completed document with the steering committee and Associate Provost Scharff, we crossed ourselves, crossed our fingers, and clicked "submit."

In December 2014, UNM received notification that the institution was not awarded the classification for the 2015 application cycle. Although I continued to emphasize to my campus that this outcome did not necessarily reflect UNM's commitment to community, the decision certainly inspired a period of self-reflection. What were we missing? Where were the gaps? The self-study itself galvanized leadership to take action and initialize steps toward a positive outcome in 2020. The feedback provided by the Carnegie National Advisory Panel was a first step in actualizing that commitment.

In February 2015, we received concrete suggestions about why UNM was not awarded the designation and were provided recommendations about how we could strengthen our community engagement agenda. Generally, the advisory board felt that there were significant issues around tracking and assessing our community engagement activities and measuring institutional impact and outcomes. Additionally, the absence of explicit support for community-engaged scholarship in our promotion and tenure policies was another significant weakness. The advisory panel suggested that the plans set forth in the UNM 2020 strategic plan were strong, and that we should use those as reference points to put us on a clearer trajectory to institutionalizing community engagement. Key points mentioned in our call included the following:

- the need to increase faculty involvement and encourage faculty to see community-engaged work as a core element of their academic work (teaching, research, and service) at our institution;
- the need to increase number of SL and community based courses available to students;
- the need to offer professional development opportunities to faculty around community-engaged teaching and research;
- the need to create new standards for tenure and promotion (in order to attract the faculty we want to attract *and* create an environment where they can thrive);
- the need to create learning objectives and outcomes (assessment) around community-based teaching and learning; and
- the need to enlist visible and vocal support from senior administration (provost, deans, chairs).

Rethinking Institutional Pathways and Policies for Engagement: Goals for 2020

UNM's acting president Chaouki Abdallah said once that universities are like giant tortoises: ancient beings that have remarkable life spans but whose evolution is so incredibly slow it is often indiscernible to the generations that pass. This evolution is responsive to external environments— economic, demographic, political, cultural, and generational. If there is one thing I have come to accept, it is that institutions of higher education are in a constant state of change, however imperceptible, and that exigency must be reflexively and iteratively embraced as opportunities arise. Both of these axioms have guided my work in rethinking UNM's pathways for engagement. With the support and awareness of the administration (provosts, deans, directors, etc.) and the faculty (faculty governance, etc.), we have been fairly systematic in our approach to addressing the limitations identified in our failed Carnegie attempt. During the past two years, we have worked toward some clear and identifiable pathways to ramp up our engagement agenda.

The UNM Community Engaged Research Lecturer Award

In 2015, with the help of our Office for the Vice President of Research, we created the annual Community Engaged Research Lecturer Award. UNM had only given one research award each year—the Annual Research Lecturer Award—since 1954. The development of the Community Engaged Research Lecturer Award was, in my opinion, a huge leap in the right direction, as it recognized the scholarly work that embodies UNM's commitment to community engagement and profoundly and systematically affects the relationship between UNM and the larger community in a positive and meaningful way. It also gave voice to and a forum for scholars whose work may have not traditionally fit into the venue of the Annual Research Lecturer Award. It is worth mentioning, however, that in two years we have had fewer than half a dozen scholars apply for the award. It is my sense that this may simply be because this is a relatively new award; however, I also realize that there are faculty who might not feel that they are ready to apply because there are institutional barriers to identifying as a community-engaged scholar (i.e., tenure and promotion policies) or that they are midcareer scholars who believe that their body of work is not of the quality expected by the award. It could also be that some scholars do not self-identify as community-engaged scholars even though the work that they do clearly fits those parameters. In short, I have come to realize that the creation of a top-level research award is not enough. Further work must be done to encourage scholars to apply and encourage deans, directors, and others to support these scholars early in their careers. Additionally, the evaluation of applicants has proven to be a work in progress. The Research Policy Committee, which is a subcommittee of our Faculty Senate, is the entity that evaluates applicants and makes recommendations for the award. Members of this committee have had to make significant changes in the way they view scholarship in order to fully understand what distinguishes a community-engaged scholar's portfolio of work from a more traditional scholarly portfolio. We are currently working to revise the rubric for evaluating applicants, and I suspect that this rubric will go through multiple iterations as we move forward with this award.

Rethinking Our Institutional Center for Community Engagement

As mentioned before, institutional support structures for engagement at UNM were heavily siloed and often did not work together to support faculty, students, and community partners doing SL or community-based research.

In 2016, the RSLP was revised into the Office for Community Engaged Learning and Research (CERL) to serve as an interdisciplinary, university-wide office committed to supporting community-engaged scholarship and teaching. We also formed the UNM Service-Learning Advisory Board (affectionately referred to as the SLAB and comprising faculty, students, staff, and community partners) to provide guidance and develop recommendations for strengthening service-based learning opportunities integrated with academic instruction. The SLAB meets several times a semester and facilitates discussion, gathers relevant data, recognizes achievement, and promotes best practices in individual courses and degree programs that choose to integrate SL or community-based research into the student experience. Although still technically housed in University College, efforts are currently underway to merge CERL with the CEC, which is currently in student affairs, and to move that merged entity under the umbrella of academic affairs. This, we believe, will create a more visible and accessible institutional center and will assist us in supporting multiple stakeholders interested in doing engaged work. Additionally, we will use this center as a resource for faculty, students, and community partners by hosting forums, seminars, and workshops to increase the quality and quantity of community-engaged teaching and research activities on our campus.

Service-Learning Course Designation and Assessment

In 2015, we developed the Service-Learning Course Designation process, which allows faculty to self-identify their courses as SL or community-based research courses. We developed definitions for both and two separate criteria for SL and community-based research because we discovered that some courses moved beyond the basic definition of offering students the opportunity to apply course knowledge and skills while working with a community partner versus conducting collaborative community-based participatory research with a community organization. We also worked with our enrollment management staff to create a course "tag" in Banner (our enrollment management system) so that students could easily discern whether a course was SL or had a community-based research component to it.

Although this effort was well intentioned, it has proven to be yet another work in progress. First, we have discovered that many faculty might be doing something like SL or community-based research, but most do not identify based on these definitions. Also, getting the word out to faculty has required a multilevel approach through campus-wide e-mail announcements, presentations to deans and directors, and reaching out department by department, which requires considerable human resources. We have also realized that we had to rethink the "apply" and "approve" language for these course designations as we do not necessarily want to be viewed as "gatekeepers" for the designation. This might intimidate or thwart faculty in seeking or understanding the benefit of the designation process. Additionally, we realized that, despite our best efforts, word of such an opportunity does not always reach faculty through the normal channels of communication. This past academic year we have taken a back-door approach and employed a graduate student to go through the course catalog and identify courses that might fit the basic criteria. With this new list, we can approach faculty and ask them if we might be able to designate their courses. Finally, we are working with the SLAB this year to develop a set of institution-wide SL course outcomes that faculty can include in their syllabi. These include both student learning outcomes and community partner outcomes. Our goal is to effectively crowdsource this information broadly enough so that we can begin measuring student outcomes and community outcomes. This, we accept, is going to take a considerable amount of time and effort before it gains traction.

Civic & Community Engagement Minor

In the fall of 2017, we implemented UNM's Civic & Community Engagement Minor (CIVCEM) of study, an 18-credit-hour interdisciplinary degree offered through University College designed to provide students with the skills and creativity to solve problems within their own communities and to develop students' own sense of self and collective efficacy and activism. The CIVCEM program was designed to give students the opportunity to build their civic agency as well as their interpersonal, leadership, and advocacy skills such as critical analysis, appreciation for diversity, and enhanced understanding of community issues and changes, and its distinctive pedagogy will integrate classroom learning with experiential and community-engaged learning opportunities, including SL, extended field study, and civic engagement at the local, national, and global levels.

Guidelines for Evaluating Community-Engaged Scholarship in Tenure and Promotion

As pointed out during our debriefing with the New England Resource Center for Higher Education (NERCHE), one thing UNM lacked was our own institutional conception and strategy for community-engaged scholarship, a broad awareness of our many efforts and the overarching framework into which they fit, and a strategic plan for advancing this aspect of our institutional mission. In April 2016, I formed the Community-Engaged Scholarship in Tenure and Promotion (CES T&P) Working Group. The charge of this ad hoc group was to draft language for policies and guidelines in the *Faculty Handbook* so that community-engaged scholarship would be explicitly identified and permitted as a mechanism for advancement, tenure, promotion, posttenure review, and merit pay decisions. The working group comprises one representative (a tenured member of the faculty) from each school or college and one representative from the Academic Freedom and Tenure Committee. The working group met several times over the course of a year. Early on, we spent a considerable amount of time ramping up our own understanding of community-engaged scholarship and educating ourselves on what other institutions were doing. We invited KerryAnn O'Meara, a noted scholar on the topic of faculty rewards and incentives, to the university to deliver a lecture and serve as a consultant and guide in this process. Our goals were lofty. Within a 12-month period we endeavored to do the following:

- Define *engaged scholarship* to permit consideration for promotion and tenure in each department and personnel document.
- Modify the *Faculty Handbook* so that community-engaged scholarship is explicitly permitted in promotion and tenure decisions as one mechanism for advancement.
- Examine all departmental and college performance review standards to gain an understanding of the number of units that have considered community-engaged scholarship in promotion and tenure decisions.
- Work with departments, schools, and colleges to identify and develop metrics and measures of engagement that are applicable to their specific units and/or disciplines.

This process proved to be one of the most challenging and frustrating of my experience. Although UNM's Academic Freedom and Tenure Committee's (AF&T) main function is to hear appeals regarding tenure and sabbatical decisions, they are also charged with reviewing tenure and promotion (T&P) policy from time to time and recommending appropriate changes. After a year of research and formulation, the working group sent its handbook language recommendations to the AF&T committee in early 2017. We received a response from the chair of AF&T that—although they respected the suggested changes—the committee had opted not to adopt them in full for the handbook updates.

As previously mentioned, I see "no" as an opportunity to forge a path to "yes." Although the AF&T committee is a formidable gatekeeper, I also know that they serve at the pleasure of the voting faculty. Over the next year, our goal is to formally see community-engaged scholarship recognized in institutional policy language. To achieve this, we must approach changes in tenure and promotion policy for community-engaged scholarship as a grassroots effort. With the working group's approval, we reframed our community-engaged scholarship T&P policy recommendations as a set of evaluation *guidelines*. We presented these guidelines to our senior vice provost for academic affairs and our associate provost for faculty development, and they recommended the following steps:

- We will circulate this draft to the Deans' Council for feedback. The message to the deans will be that the goal is not policy change but rather the goal of academic affairs is to put these guidelines forward as a *recommendation* for consideration by all colleges, schools, and departments for adoption and incorporation into departmental T&P guidelines.
- For further due diligence, we will also post these drafted guidelines on the provost's website as an academic initiative, requesting feedback from campus-wide stakeholders.
- Once we get feedback and comment from the campus community, our goal will be to post these guidelines on the Office for Faculty Affairs & Services (OFAS) website.
- In fall 2017, our goal will be to do a "road show" with departments to discuss and recommend ways that each can incorporate these guidelines into their own departmental evaluation policies.

Conclusions

Not receiving the Carnegie designation was disappointing. But, in retrospect, the process proved beneficial in that it allowed us to deepen our commitment to the work we were already doing through policy and practice. It also offered us the opportunity to identify gaps in our institutional identity. Although I fully recognize that this chapter speaks little about the role of community partners in institutionalizing community engagement, readers must accept this limitation as evidence that UNM is diligently working toward knowing ourselves first as an institution and, more importantly, what structural elements need to be in place so that we can truly be an engaged institution. Additionally, not receiving the designation allowed me the opportunity as the lead strategic planner for community engagement to learn more about the history that has thwarted change in the past, the bureaucratic barriers that exist and that impact future change, the exemplary work being done by faculty and departments in concert with and in benefit to the community, and, finally, identify and develop a cadre of stalwart advocates for community engagement around campus and our community.

Chapter Fourteen

KEY LESSONS AND GUIDING QUESTIONS

The Process of Gathering and Using Evidence

Georgina Manok

Create Robust Data Collection and Selection Systems

The data collection and evidence-gathering process is one of the most important elements of the Carnegie Community Engagement Classification. The classification asks for evidence that is generated through "systematic assessment." The point is not to collect data solely for classification but to have systems in place that collect data on an ongoing basis that can be used for the application. Your campus will likely have a number of offices that can provide useful information for your classification, and filtering and selecting data may be one of the most challenging elements of the classification application. There are word limits so you need to be strategically selective and choose data points to highlight your best practice. It is important to be able to tell your institutional community engagement story while being able to back it up with evidence. A key lesson here is wide involvement in data collection. This includes creating subcommittees and possibly specific data collection committees. Some guiding questions include the following:

- Are we investing in a strong and sustainable relationship with the institutional research office or other offices or individuals charged with institutional assessment?
- Who are we involving in data collection and are we missing any key players?

Avoid engaging other units on campus only as a one-time service or data provider.

Upgrade Your Assessment Tools

As you work on establishing a sustainable and strong relationship with your institutional research office and key offices on campus, it is essential to identify all data needs. You can then ask your institutional research office to aggregate data across relevant instruments and assessment tools that your campus utilizes. You can also use the time between classification and re-classification to establish new data collection frameworks and adopt new instruments. One example is utilizing the National Assessment for Service and Community Engagement ecosystem of tools and the National Infrastructure Inventory for Community Engagement, which both align with the classification applications. Some guiding questions include the following:

- How can we introduce edits to existing instruments to feed into the application framework?
- Are we involving community partners in our data collection process?
- What instruments are being developed in the field, and are other peers developing and using them to track progress and collect data?

Avoid shying away from your weaknesses or data collection caveats. Describe them and your plans of remedying them.

Look for Synergies With Other Self-Studies

The data collection involved in the Carnegie Community Engagement Classification process is very useful in other self-studies. The type of data you are collecting may be done for the first time or consolidated in a particular way that your institution has not done before. This will be very valuable as you navigate institutional accreditations. Hence, building synergies between your classification process and accreditation processes will add value to your community engagement efforts and increase the motivation for leadership endorsement. Some guiding questions include the following:

- Are we involving someone who chairs or is knowledgeable about institutional accreditations in our core team?
- What can we learn from our reaccreditation processes to inform our re-classification process and vice versa?

Avoid treating the Carnegie Community Engagement Classification as a stand-alone project and try to create synergies with other institutional review and improvement processes.

AFTERWORD

So You're Carnegie Classified; Now What?

Georgina Manok

And when you have reached the mountain top, then you shall begin to climb.

—Kahlil Gibran, *The Prophet*, 1923

The application process for the Carnegie Community Engagement Classification has a multitude of impacts on participating institutions. As presented in the diverse campus experiences in this volume, the classification application has acted as a baseline for community engagement commitments. It has highlighted key development needs for campuses that were later embedded in institutional strategic plans. The process has contributed to institutional learning and collection of data that may have never been consolidated before. It has preserved institutional stability across campuses in times of leadership change. The classification has encouraged campuses to develop and upgrade data collection tools, instruments, and processes and has been used to guide recruitment searches. The classification has also helped campus leaders find key ingredients as they build community engagement centers and engaged initiatives in their institutions. From moderate to transformational institutional change, the classification (and commitment to re-classification) has encouraged and guided campuses as they create sustainable, lasting, reciprocal, and mutually beneficial community partnerships across all campus constituencies.

The Carnegie Classification is one tool for campuses to use to assess their community engagement commitments and advance an engagement agenda. As the administrative home of the classification, the Swearer Center for Public Service at Brown University, we encourage campuses to use the Carnegie Classification as one in a menu of tools and instruments that are available for assessing community engagement. In particular, we encourage campuses to employ various assessments in the years between classification and re-classification, both as a way of continuing a process of assessment for improvement and as a way of creating an evidence base toward successful re-classification. One such tool, for example, also housed at the Swearer Center, that we continue to develop in collaboration with Campus Compact and Siena College, is the National Assessment of Service and Community Engagement (NASCE). The NASCE provides an ecosystem of survey instruments to measure and track the depth and breadth of student, faculty, and staff engagement on campuses. Because classification happens every 10 years, we would like campuses to find ways to continue the assessment process in the intervening years.

For Those of You Who Received the Classification, Now What?

Your classification is a moment to plan what the next chapter of community engagement looks like on your campus. Because you have committed yourself to being recognized for your work in community engagement, although your campus story, experience, motivations, and process may be unique, there are many lessons you can learn from peer campuses highlighted in this volume. A common thread suggests cementing the recognition of the classification through embedding community engagement in the strategic direction and planning for your institution for the decade to follow, which can be broken down into 1-year, 5-year, and 10-year plans. This can be solidified by creating documents that reflect your strategic objectives and how and why you plan to engage with community partners and present your campus as an anchor of community engagement.

As you plan for the re-classification, our webpage offers valuable resources to support you. These include frequently asked questions about the application, webinars, and publications (Brown University, 2016). Another important element of our resource page is the successful first-time and re-classification samples from earlier classification cycles. Several campuses highlighted in this volume have made public their successful applications. Although your campus experience may be unique, you will benefit from the type of evidence provided by institutions and from seeing how the process described in their chapters maps to their actual applications.

The self-assessment process is an opportunity to deeply review and reflect on your institutional infrastructure, practices, and value for engagement. Use the momentum that comes with the classification announcement to create sustainable infrastructures and to educate your campus about the importance of the classification and your commitment to it. Continue to collect data and upgrade your evidence-gathering tools and instruments and review progress toward promises you've made to the framework.

The Carnegie Community Engagement Classification is not static; it is a dynamic instrument. The framework has evolved with time to incorporate new and emerging trends in the field, bridge gaps in existing practices, and encourage campuses to adopt institutional changes that will facilitate and sustain community engagement. As administrators of the classification, our work on the classification framework is an ongoing endeavor. We work with field leaders, scholars, practitioners, and community engagement networks to continuously advance the field. Our College and University Engagement Initiative (CUEI), of which this classification is a major component, aims to convene key players including Campus Compact and networks in the field to advance community engagement in higher education and embed community engagement in research, scholarship, and action across campuses. As we continue to develop and refine the classification framework to follow key trends in the field, new components will be added to the application framework.

We hope you find a useful resource in the campus experiences compiled in this book. We look forward to collaborating with you on your journey toward transformational institutional change and the advancement of teaching, learning, and research, while also nurturing their broader impacts.

Georgina Manok
Brown University

Reference

Brown University. (2016). *Swearer Center.* Retrieved from https://www.brown .edu/academics/college/swearer

Editors

John Saltmarsh is professor of higher education in the Department of Leadership in Education in the College of Education and Human Development at the University of Massachusetts, Boston. He is also distinguished engaged scholar at the Swearer Center for Public Service at Brown University, where he leads the project in which the Swearer Center serves as the administrative partner with the Carnegie Foundation for Elective Community Engagement Classification.

Mathew B. Johnson is associate dean for engaged scholarship and executive director of the Howard R. Swearer Center for Public Service at Brown University, Providence. The Swearer Center is home of the College and University Engagement Initiative, which includes the administration of the Carnegie Community Engagement Classification, the National Assessment for Service and Community Engagement, the Lynton Early Career Faculty Award for Engaged Scholarship, and other field-building projects and initiatives.

Contributors

Lina D. Dostilio is the assistant vice chancellor of community engagement and associate professor of practice of education at the University of Pittsburgh. In this capacity she is leading the University of Pittsburgh's strategic initiative on place-based community engagement. Dostilio is also the scholar in residence for Campus Compact, leading the research initiative on the community engagement professional in higher education, and also serves on the editorial board of *Metropolitan Universities*.

Julie A. Hatcher is the executive director of Indiana University–Purdue University Indianapolis's (IUPUI's) Center for Service and Learning and associate professor of philanthropic studies at the Lilly Family School of Philanthropy at IUPUI. Her research focuses on the role of higher education in civil society, civic learning, outcomes in higher education, and the philanthropic motivations of professionals. She is the 2017 recipient of the Distinguished Career Award through the International Association for Research on Service-Learning and Community Engagement. She serves on the National Advisory Board for the Carnegie Elective Classification for Community Engagement.

Stephen P. Hundley is professor of organizational leadership at IUPUI, where he also serves as senior adviser to the chancellor for planning and institutional improvement. He writes, consults, and presents on topics related to organizational effectiveness, learning and development strategies, and higher education administration. He is chair of the Assessment Institute in Indianapolis, now the nation's oldest and largest event focused on outcomes assessment in higher education, and is executive editor of *Assessment Update.*

Emily M. Janke is the founding director of the Institute for Community and Economic Engagement and an associate professor in the Department of Peace and Conflict Studies at the University of North Carolina at Greensboro. The institute promotes and contributes to the scholarship of community engagement within UNCG and beyond through pursuing active research and scholarship, supporting institutional strategic initiatives, and providing professional development opportunities. Emily serves on the National Advisory Panel of the Carnegie Foundation's Community Engagement Elective Classification, the University of North Carolina Engagement Council, and on the editorial boards of the *Journal of Higher Education Outreach and Engagement* and *Metropolitan Universities Journal.*

Richard Kiely serves as senior fellow in the Office of Engagement Initiatives as part of Engaged Cornell and is an adjunct professor in the Department of City and Regional Planning at Cornell University. Previously, he was director of Engaged Learning and Research and faculty director of the Urban Scholars Program at Cornell University. He is currently leading an effort to evaluate the impact of Engaged Cornell, a large-scale community engagement initiative at Cornell University. As the cofounder of the field-building website globalsl.org and the coeditor of two special sections on global service-learning for the *Michigan Journal of Community Service Learning*, Richard continues to be an active scholar in the area of service-learning and community engagement and regularly conducts workshops for students, staff, and faculty on course design, critical reflection, (global) service-learning, assessment, and program evaluation.

Amanda Kittelberger has spent a career working across education-related fields including teaching and learning, community engagement, and state education policy. She served most recently as a senior staff member at Cornell University supporting projects and initiatives within the Provost Office, and is currently living in Zomba, Malawi, where she is building local interest and capacity in community-engaged learning.

Monica Kowal is associate dean for community engaged learning and research at the University of New Mexico, where she also serves as strategic planner for community engagement in the Office of the Provost and senior vice president for academic affairs. Her primary responsibilities are planning and directing institutional strategic and long-range goals for community engagement and providing research, planning, and leadership in the development of core community engagement programs and initiatives. She is vice chair on the board of the International Association for Research on Service-Learning and Community Engagement (IARSLCE) and serves as an associate editor for the *Journal of Experiential Education*. She is also cochair of the Emerging Engagement Scholars Workshop (EESW) with the Engagement Scholarship Consortium (ESC), a professional development workshop for advanced doctoral students and early career faculty. Her research interests include service-learning curriculum and assessment, faculty development in service-learning course design, and the institutionalization of community engagement at minority-serving institutions in the United States.

Brenda Marsteller Kowalewski is associate provost for high-impact programs and faculty development at Weber State University, Ogden, Utah. In addition to overseeing centers for community engagement, undergraduate research, and sustainability practices and research, Kowalewski is responsible for coordinating the university's community development efforts. She is chair of the Ogden Civic Action Network (OgdenCAN) steering committee, which coordinates a coalition of seven anchor institutions focused on housing, health, and education challenges in the East Central Ogden neighborhood and serves on the planning committee for the Coalition of Urban and Metropolitan Universities (CUMU).

Georgina Manok is manager of research and assessment at the Swearer Center for Public Service at Brown University. She designs and implements center-wide and programmatic assessment and evaluation strategies, and contributes to the center's curricular, cocurricular, and community engagement programming. Georgina is a core member of the center's

College and University Engagement Initiative (CUEI), which convenes a community of local and international higher education institutions to collaborate on research, institutional development, and programming related to community engagement and innovation.

Marisol Morales is the founding director of the Office of Civic and Community Engagement at the University of La Verne, a four-year comprehensive Hispanic-serving institution (HSI) located in Southern California. She has served in this role since 2013, and she is responsible for leading and developing university-community engagement initiatives in the area of academic service-learning, community-engaged scholarship, and cocurricular community engagement. She is a board member of the International Association for Research on Service Learning and Community Engagement (IARSLCE). Prior to joining the University of La Verne, she was the associate director at the Steans Center for Community-Based Service Learning and Community Service Studies at DePaul University. She is currently pursuing a doctoral degree in organizational leadership at the University of La Verne.

Melissa Quan is director of the Center for Faith and Public Life at Fairfield University, where she has worked since 2002. Her responsibilities include leading the institutionalization of service-learning at Fairfield University and managing several community-based research projects. Melissa completed her master's degree in education at Fairfield University with a concentration on service-learning and civic engagement in 2005 and is currently pursuing a doctoral degree in higher education at the University of Massachusetts Boston.

John Reiff is director of civic learning and engagement for the Massachusetts Department of Higher Education, where he helps public colleges and universities implement a first-in-the-nation policy calling on the commonwealth's public higher education institutions to involve all of their undergraduates in civic learning—in the classroom, in the cocurriculum, and in engagement with communities beyond the campus. From 2000 to 2016 he was director of civic engagement and service-learning at the University of Massachusetts Amherst.

Marshall Welch serves on the Executive Board of the International Association for Research on Service-Learning and Community Engagement (IARSLCE). Previously he was the assistant vice provost for community engagement and the director of the Catholic Institute for Lasallian

Social Action (CILSA) at Saint Mary's College of California and the director of the Lowell Bennion Community Service Center at the University of Utah. He is the author of *Engaging Higher Education: Purpose, Platforms, and Programs for Community Engagement* (Stylus Publishing, 2016). He is the coauthor of the National Inventory of Institutional Infrastructure for Community Engagement (NIIICE) and an independent scholar living in the Portland, Oregon, area.

Amanda Wittman is an associate director in the Office of Engagement Initiatives at Cornell University. She works with faculty to develop community-engaged courses and curricula and has an abiding interest in evaluation, assessment, and measurement.

constituencies—students, faculty, communities, and institutions; and discussion of strategies for data collection, analysis, synthesis, and reporting. Specific assessment instruments for use with each constituency are provided, including suggestions for administration, preparation, and data analysis. This volume will be helpful for individuals seeking a comprehensive resource on assessment issues in higher education.

Campus Compact

45 Temple Place
Boston, MA 02111

Subscribe to our newsletter: https://compact.org

The Community Engagement Professional in Higher Education

A Competency Model for an Emerging Field

Edited by Lina D. Dostilio

Foreword by Andrew J. Seligoshn

"This book illuminates important work of thinly acknowledged citizens of academe—community engaged professionals. It advances the movement for publicly engaged scholarship giving voice to their person, place, and purpose in academe with myriad inflections beyond campus borders." **Timothy Eatman**, *Associate Professor, Syracuse University, Director for Research for Imagining America (IA)*

This book, offered by practitioner-scholars, is an exploration and identification of the knowledge, skills, and dispositions that are central to supporting effective community engagement practices between higher education and communities. The discussion and review of these core competencies are framed within a broader context of the changing landscape of institutional community engagement and the emergence of the community engagement professional as a facilitator of engaged teaching, research, and institutional partnerships distinct from other academic professionals.

Assessing Service-Learning and Civic Engagement (Second Edition)

Principles and Techniques

Sherril B. Gelmon, Barbara A. Holland and Amy Spring

With Seanna Kerrigan and Amy Driscoll

This book offers a broad overview of many issues related to assessment in higher education, with specific application for understanding the impact of service-learning and civic engagement initiatives. This revised edition includes an additional chapter which explores recent changes in the assessment landscape and offers examples and resources for designing assessment strategies for community engagement in higher education. The original text includes narrative addressing assessment issues and strategies; detailed discussion of learning from multiple research projects performed over the past two decades about impact on multiple

(Continued on preceding page)